Uncovering Your TRUE SAGE:

A Guided Journey Back To Your Truest Self

Rediscover the wisdom that resides within! *Uncovering Your TRUE SAGE* is not just an oracle card deck–it's a profound journey into the depths of your authentic self.

Each card in this deck is a gateway to deeper self-awareness, designed to guide you through the layers of your being and illuminate the path to your truest essence. Whether you seek clarity, healing, or a renewed connection to your inner wisdom, these cards offer insights and exercises that resonate with the core of who you are.

Whether you are new to oracle cards or an experienced practitioner, this deck invites you to embark on a transformative journey back to the heart of your being. Let each card be a beacon of light, guiding you home to your truest self.

Are you ready to uncover the sage within?

INTRODUCTION

Welcome to the Uncovering your TRUE SAGE Oracle Card Deck. Uncovering Your TRUE SAGE: A Guided Journey Back To Your Truest Self and Rediscover the Wisdom That Resides Within!

Uncovering Your TRUE SAGE is not just an oracle card deck–it's an addition tool on your profound journey into the depths of your authentic self. Each card in this deck is a gateway to deeper self-awareness, designed to guide you through the layers of your being and illuminate the path to your truest essence. The more positive things you do to improve your life, the better.

In addition to counseling, collaborating with helpful professionals, and always being open as well as following through with the people and resources to help you on your journey, the hope is that these cards can enhance your journey.

Whether you seek clarity, healing, or a renewed connection to your inner wisdom, these cards offer insights and exercises that can resonate with the core of who you are. Whether you are new to oracle cards or an experienced practitioner, this deck invites you to enjoy your transformative journey back to the heart of your being.

This deck was created to be a powerful tool to guide you on your journey of introspection, healing, growth, and transformation. Each card serves as a mirror, reflecting aspects of your inner world and offering insights to enhance your understanding of yourself and your path in life.

My name is Dr. Brian Alman, and I'm the Founder, Clinical Director, and CEO of True Sage. My company provides stress management strategies through my proven ACE (Adverse Childhood Experiences) treatment solutions to empower people to become their own True Sage.

As a longtime practitioner with my PhD in clinical psychology who has worked with professionals from many disciplines, companies, athletes, stress management groups, and people from many countries with challenges that include anxiety, depression, weight, addictions, health problems and more, I've learned that so much of how we deal with life's ups and downs as adults comes from the experiences–both good and bad–that we had as children.

Not only are our behaviors and habits influenced by the experiences in our childhood, but our physical health, too. The Adverse Childhood Experiences (ACE) assessment and Positive Childhood Experiences (PCE) assessment – (in the back of this booklet in the "Resources" section) will give you a score of 0 to 10. Learning how to utilize your positive experiences to help you with adversity has been proven to be beneficial. The ACE Study showed a correlation between one's ACE Score and their likelihood of developing physical and mental difficulties –including anxiety, depression – and more in adulthood. This correlation emphasizes that while the adverse experiences stay in the past, their effects on us can remain and impact our future if left unresolved.

This deck can help you develop the more tools to handle life's stressors, manage your emotions, and cultivate inner resilience and self-acceptance so that your positive childhood experiences can be utilized even more to help you integrate your potential for a future of freedom, fulfillment, joy and become your best True Sage.

THE PURPOSE OF THIS DECK

This deck supports your healing, personal development, and self-awareness. It is a tool to help you connect with your intuition, gain clarity on your thoughts and emotions, and discover deeper layers of your being. By using these cards regularly, you can cultivate a greater sense of presence, purpose, and peace in your life.

THE EXERCISES

Each card comes with a related exercise, affirmation, or prompt to help you break free of old patterns and guide you toward healing and growth. The exercises are clinically proven, and I've created and used them in my practice for decades, starting with when I worked directly with Dr. Vincent Felitti, the Co-Principal Investigator of the ACE Study I mentioned earlier. While these exercises have been curated to fit the corresponding card's topic, their application is incredibly versatile. I encourage you to save your favorites and make them a habit.

ORACLE CARDS

ACCEPTANCE

The Acceptance card embodies the power of embracing reality as it is without resistance or judgment. It symbolizes the willingness to acknowledge and make peace with the present moment, including its joys and challenges. This card invites us to surrender to what is, release the need for control, and open our hearts to the profound wisdom and healing that comes with acceptance.

Key Meanings:

Surrender and Letting Go: Acceptance invites us to surrender to the flow of life, releasing the need to control or manipulate outcomes. This card reminds us that there is freedom and peace in letting go of resistance and embracing the natural unfolding of events.
By surrendering to what is, we open ourselves to the infinite possibilities and blessings that await us each moment.

Self-Acceptance and Compassion: Acceptance begins with accepting ourselves exactly as we are, with all our flaws, imperfections, and vulnerabilities. This card encourages us to cultivate self-acceptance and self-compassion, recognizing that we are worthy of love and belonging just as we are. By embracing our whole selves with kindness and understanding, we can heal the wounds of self-judgment and shame and experience a deep sense of inner peace.

Embracing Impermanence: Acceptance is rooted in the understanding that everything in life is impermanent and that change is the only constant. This card reminds us that clinging to the past or worrying about the future only leads to stress and that true peace can be found by fully embracing the present moment. By accepting the impermanence of life, we can let go of attachment and find freedom.

Forgiveness and Reconciliation: Acceptance also involves forgiving ourselves and others for past mistakes and transgressions. This card invites us to let go of resentment, bitterness, and blame, recognizing that grudges only perpetuate suffering. By practicing forgiveness and reconciliation,
we free ourselves from the burden of the past and open ourselves up to
the possibility of healing.

Takeaway:

Embrace reality as it is and surrender to the flow of life. Cultivate acceptance of yourself, others, and the circumstances of your life, knowing that true peace and freedom lie in letting go of resistance and opening your heart to the wisdom and healing that comes with acceptance. Embrace the journey of surrender and acceptance, and watch as you experience a profound sense of peace, wholeness, and liberation.

Exercise:

Letting Go

Here's an exact breathing method so you can let go and find relaxation anytime.

The next time you feel stress building inside–whether you're pressured at work or running out of time–simply close your eyes and turn your attention to your breathing. Feel the expanding and contracting of your lungs as you get into the rhythm of your inhales and exhales. Don't try to change your breathing pattern; simply acknowledge how it is and follow it.

Whether your breathing is deep or shallow, nose or mouth, fast or slow, just accept your breathing as it is. There's nothing to do right; there's nothing you can do wrong. Again, just focus on your breathing and accept it as it is.

It's like looking up at the clouds floating across the sky or watching the waves at the beach rolling in and rolling out. Just accept your breathing however it is. After just a few breaths, you'll be in a more relaxed and comfortable state, and your stress will have gotten so small it may have disappeared entirely.

Practice these let-go breaths daily, even if just for a moment before you turn on your computer or sit down for dinner. This exercise is also a starting point to many of the others in this book. Soon, you'll come to trust that with more awareness and acceptance, you can breathe your way through anything.

Letting Go in 5 Easy Steps

1. Close your eyes and turn your attention to your breathing.
2. Get into the rhythm of your breath without trying to change it.
3. Accept your breathing as it is.
4. Focus on your breath.
5. After a few minutes, note how you feel. Has your breathing normalized?

ACE (ADVERSE CHILDHOOD EXPERIENCES)

The ACE Study, conducted by the Centers for Disease Control and Prevention (CDC) and Kaiser Permanente in the late 1990s, examined the correlation between adverse childhood experiences and long-term health outcomes. The study identified ten types of adverse childhood experiences, including abuse, neglect, and household dysfunction, and found a strong association between the number of ACEs a person experienced and their risk for various physical and mental health conditions later in life. The ACE Study highlighted the importance of addressing childhood trauma and promoting resilience as key factors in preventing and mitigating the impact of adverse experiences on health and well-being.

The ACEs card sheds light on the impact of Adverse Childhood Experiences (ACEs) on our lives and well-being. It symbolizes recognizing and acknowledging past traumas or challenges that may continue to affect us into adulthood. This card invites us to explore and heal from these experiences, recognizing that our resilience and ability to thrive are not defined by our past but shaped by our capacity for healing and growth.

Key Meanings:

Acknowledgment and Awareness: The ACEs card encourages acknowledgment and awareness of the adverse childhood experiences that may have shaped our lives.

This card reminds us that by shining a light on our past traumas or challenges, we can begin the process of healing and transformation. By acknowledging the impact of these experiences on our lives, we empower ourselves to break free from their grip and reclaim our sense of agency and wholeness.

Healing and Transformation: ACEs symbolize the journey of healing and transformation from past wounds. This card invites us to explore and heal from the pain and trauma of our past, recognizing that healing is not a linear process but a journey of self-discovery and growth. By embracing our wounds with compassion and courage, we create space for healing and transformation to occur, allowing us to break free from the cycle of trauma and step into a life of greater resilience and wholeness.

Building Resilience: The ACEs card reminds us of our innate resilience–the capacity to overcome adversity and thrive in the face of challenges. This card invites us to cultivate resilience by nurturing our emotional well-being, seeking support from trusted others, and practicing self-care and self-compassion. By building resilience, we strengthen our ability to cope with life's ups and downs and create a foundation for lasting healing and growth.

Breaking the Cycle: ACEs represent the opportunity to break the cycle of intergenerational trauma and create a brighter future for ourselves and future generations. This card reminds us that healing from adverse childhood experiences is not only about our own well-being but about creating a ripple effect of healing and transformation in our families and communities. By doing the inner work of healing, we contribute to the collective healing of humanity and pave the way for a future rooted in resilience, compassion, and joy.

Takeaway:

The ACEs card highlights the adverse childhood experiences that may have impacted our lives. It signifies the importance of acknowledging, understanding, and healing from these past traumas or challenges to reclaim our power and well-being. This card invites us to embark on a journey of self-discovery, healing, and resilience as we confront and transcend the wounds of our past.

Exercise:

Take the ACE Assessment to determine your ACE Score. It is available in the "Resources" section of this book.

Be sure to take a moment to reflect and answer the final questions, which are extremely helpful in beginning to resolve trauma associated with adverse childhood experiences and stopping their negative effect on your life.

ADVICE (FOR YOURSELF)

The Advice card serves as a gentle reminder to turn inward and seek guidance from your own inner wisdom. It symbolizes the power of self-reflection, introspection, and self-trust in decision making and navigating life's challenges. This card invites you to pause, listen to the whispers of your heart, and trust the insights and nudges that arise from within.

Key Meanings:

Self-Reflection and Contemplation: The Advice card encourages you to take time for self-reflection and contemplation, to pause and connect with your innermost thoughts and feelings. The answers you seek are often found within yourself, waiting to be discovered through quiet introspection. By carving out moments of stillness and silence, you create space for clarity to emerge.

Trusting Your Inner Wisdom: Trust the wisdom that resides within you–that innate knowing. This card reminds you that you are your own best advisor, and that you have access to a vast reservoir of wisdom and insight within yourself. By trusting the nudges and insights that arise from within, you can navigate life's challenges with confidence and clarity.

Honoring Your Truth: The Advice card encourages you to honor your truth and authenticity in all areas of your life. This card reminds you that only you know what is truly best for you, and that it is important to trust your instincts and follow your inner guidance, even if it diverges from the expectations or opinions of others. By honoring your truth and authenticity, you can create a life that is in harmony with your deepest values and aspirations.

Taking Inspired Action: Self-reflection and introspection are not passive activities, but rather opportunities to gain clarity and insight that can inform your decisions and actions moving forward. By taking aligned action based on your inner guidance, you empower yourself to create the life you desire with confidence and conviction.

Takeaway:

Turn inward and seek guidance from your own innate wisdom. Trust the insights and nudges that arise from within, and take inspired action based on the guidance you receive. Embrace the power of self-reflection and introspection, and watch as you navigate life's challenges with clarity, confidence, and grace.

Exercise:

Journaling with Dominant and Non-Dominant Hand

Although we cannot change the past (no matter how much we'd like to), we can continue to grow from it, despite it. Like a tree with many rings, each ring indicating the tree's age must grow upon the last. You cannot cut the center, younger rings if the tree is to survive and thrive into the future. That's the way it is.

Like a tree, we keep growing–our inner rings are part of us, but they do not define us, nor are they the newest, evolved version of ourselves.

To cultivate inner guidance and advice, try journaling with both your dominant and non-dominant hands, where your non-dominant hand is the past version of yourself and the present you is represented by your dominant hand.

When doing your non-dominant hand journaling, allow your non-dominant hand to express your past problems, difficulties, trauma, and pain, as well as the lessons and wisdom imparted by those experiences. Then, switch to your dominant hand. Write, draw, or doodle the here and now, the spontaneous, the intuitive. This is the present you. The dominant you. Allow any new ideas, resolutions, perspectives, images, words, or epiphanies to flow from mind to pen to paper with ease.

You can go back and forth between your non-dominant hand, your past, and your dominant hand, your present, as many times as you'd like.

Then, you're ready for the final step: A dialogue between the past and present you. The previous writing exercise may have already sparked this internal conversation. Continue, and with regular practice, this exchange will become natural and straightforward, and your present self will secure its place as dominant in your mental self-talk.

The more you allow for this kind of conversation, the more you'll be able to utilize the past as a bridge to help you get the best inner advice for yourself in the present.

ALCHEMY (MEDITATION)

The Alchemy card symbolizes transformation, transmutation, and the profound process of turning the ordinary into the extraordinary. It represents the ability to take experiences, challenges, and raw potential and transform them into something of great value and significance. This card invites you to embrace your inner alchemist, encouraging you to recognize your power to create change and manifest your highest potential.

Key Meanings:

Transformation: You can change and evolve, turning challenges and obstacles into opportunities for growth. Embrace the transformative process and trust in your capacity to create positive change.

Transmutation: Alchemy involves the transmutation of base elements into something more valuable. Look at areas of your life where you can apply this principle, transforming negative experiences, emotions, or circumstances into sources of strength and wisdom.

Creativity and Innovation: Think outside the box and use creativity to solve problems and create new possibilities. You can achieve remarkable outcomes by blending different elements of your life in innovative ways.

Manifestation: Alchemy is also about manifesting and realizing your goals and dreams. Set clear intentions and take purposeful actions to bring your visions to life–trust in manifesting your desires through focused effort and positive energy.

Takeaway:

Embrace the process of alchemy in your life, recognizing your ability to turn challenges into opportunities and manifest your highest potential. Consider how you can apply the principles of transformation, transmutation, creativity, and manifestation to your current situation.
By doing so, you can unlock your potential and achieve extraordinary outcomes.

Exercise:

Embrace Your Inner Alchemist

Turn challenges into opportunities and manifest your highest potential by reflecting and journaling. First, identify a challenge. Write about it in detail in your journal. What makes it a challenge? How does it impact you?

Then, imagine how this challenge could be transformed into a positive opportunity. Write about the potential positive outcomes that could emerge from this situation. What strengths or qualities could you develop through overcoming this challenge?

Finally, reflect on a past experience where you successfully turned a negative situation into a positive outcome. Write about what you did, how you felt during the process, and the results. What elements of that experience can you apply to your current challenge?

ANGER

Anger is not just an intense and powerful emotion that arises in response to perceived injustice, frustration, or threat. It embodies a fiery energy that, when harnessed and understood, can fuel our actions and lead to personal growth. This card invites us to explore the root causes of our anger, acknowledge and honor the emotion, and channel its energy in constructive and healing ways, thereby transforming it from a destructive force into a catalyst for positive change.

Key Meanings:

Acknowledgment and Acceptance: The Anger card encourages us to acknowledge and accept the presence of anger within ourselves. This card reminds us that anger is a natural and valid emotion. By acknowledging and accepting it, we can understand and address its underlying causes more effectively. By embracing our anger with compassion and curiosity, we can transform it from a destructive force into a catalyst for growth and change.

Exploring Triggers and Boundaries: Anger often arises in response to specific triggers or violations of our boundaries. This card invites us to explore the triggers and boundaries that contribute to our anger, whether external events or internal thought patterns. By gaining clarity about our triggers and boundaries, we can assert ourselves more effectively and navigate conflicts with greater ease and assertiveness.

Healthy Expression and Release: While anger can feel overwhelming, the Anger card reminds us that we have the power to express and release it in healthy ways. This card encourages us to find constructive outlets for our anger, such as journaling, physical exercise, or creative expression. By channeling the energy of anger into productive activities, we can release its grip on us and experience a sense of relief and empowerment.

Forgiveness and Healing: Ultimately, the Anger card calls us to practice forgiveness and healing for ourselves and others. This card invites us to release resentment, bitterness, and blame, recognizing that holding onto anger only perpetuates our suffering. By practicing forgiveness and compassion, we liberate ourselves from the grip of anger and open ourselves up to the possibility of healing and reconciliation.

Takeaway:

Explore and honor the emotion of anger within yourself. Acknowledge the triggers and boundaries that contribute to your anger, find healthy outlets for its expression, and practice forgiveness and healing as a path toward liberation. Embrace the transformative power of anger, and watch as you harness its energy to create positive change and growth in your life.

Exercise:

Say It 3 Times

Here's an easy way to make sure that you're accepting your feeling of anger rather than trying to get rid of it: Become aware of your anger and notice that it's there inside of you. Now, take a deep breath and name it slowly three times.

For example, if you're feeling angry, just notice it, breathe deeply, and say to yourself, "angry...angry...angry." Or let's say you're anxious about something, someone, yourself, others, your work, anything–just recognize it, breathe deeply, and say, "anxious... anxious... anxious."
Say it aloud or to yourself. Say it slowly three times.

By saying what you're feeling three times, you become more aware of that feeling and more present with it. And once you become more aware of the emotion, something incredible happens: The feeling loses its power. Once you're aware, conscious, and focused on its presence, you become separate from it. Soon, you're back in the present, and your stress has melted away.

Say It 3 Times in 3 Easy Steps

1. Identify what you are feeling.
2. Become aware of the feeling.
3. Take a deep breath and name it slowly three times, in your head or aloud.

ANXIETY

The Anxiety card symbolizes the overwhelming feelings of worry, fear, and unease that can grip us in times of stress or uncertainty. It embodies the mental and emotional turmoil accompanying anxious thoughts and sensations, disrupting our peace of mind and hindering our ability to function effectively. This card invites us to acknowledge and address our anxiety's root causes and cultivate practices that promote calmness, resilience, and inner peace.

Key Meanings:

Acknowledgment and Awareness: The Anxiety card encourages us to acknowledge and become aware of the feelings of anxiety that may be present within us. This card reminds us that it is okay to feel anxious and that by acknowledging our emotions, we can begin to understand and address their underlying causes. By shining a light on our anxiety, we take the first step towards healing and finding relief.

Understanding Triggers and Patterns: Anxiety often arises in response to specific triggers or patterns of thinking that exacerbate our feelings of fear and worry. This card invites us to explore the triggers and patterns that contribute to our anxiety, whether they are external stressors or internal thought patterns. By gaining insight into the root causes of our anxiety, we can begin to develop strategies for managing and overcoming it.

Cultivating Calmness and Resilience: While anxiety can feel overwhelming, the Anxiety card reminds us that we can cultivate calmness and resilience in facing our fears. This card encourages us to practice relaxation techniques such as deep breathing, meditation, or gentle movement to soothe our nervous system and quiet our racing thoughts. By developing a toolbox of coping strategies, we can navigate anxiety more effectively and build our resilience over time.

Seeking Support and Guidance: It's important to remember that we don't have to face anxiety alone. Instead, seek support and guidance from trusted friends, family members, or mental health professionals. Whether through therapy, support groups, or simply talking with loved ones, seeking support can provide us with the encouragement and validation we need to navigate our anxiety and find healing.

Takeaway:

Acknowledge and address any feelings of anxiety that may be present within you. Explore the root causes of your anxiety, develop strategies for managing it, and seek support from others when needed. Embrace the journey of healing and self-discovery, and know that with patience, compassion, and support, you can relieve anxiety and cultivate greater peace of mind and well-being.

Exercise:

Positive Self-Talk

Everyday inner self-talk plays a huge role in shaping our lives and the anxiety we experience. It's nearly impossible to let go of anxiety when continually telling ourselves things like:

"I just can't do this."
"I'll probably fail."
"I just don't like me."
"I'm no good."
"I don't know what's wrong with me."
"I'll never learn."

With anxiety, this voice is so thoroughly programmed in the brain, and sometimes these messages are all you can hear. They are continually saying things to themselves that simply aren't true–that they are not good enough, cannot help themselves, will not succeed, are not as good a person as they should, and do not deserve to be happy. This negative self-talk is what I call being tied up in 'not's,' and it's second nature for so many with anxiety.

You mustn't try to stop yourself from saying all the negatives; that would only give your Inner Critic more energy and control. Still, imagine how much more relaxed you could be if you were saying soothing, supportive, last-row things to yourself like:

"I'm making progress."
"I can handle this."
"I'm getting free of my stress."
"I'm willing to try." "I know I'll get there."

With positive self-talk, you can begin to self-soothe in high-anxiety moments.

ATTITUDE

The Attitude card symbolizes the power of our perspective and mindset in shaping our experiences and outcomes in life. It embodies our attitude towards ourselves, others, and the world. This card invites us to cultivate a positive attitude that empowers us to navigate life's challenges with resilience, optimism, and grace.

Key Meanings:

Optimism and Hope: Attitude represents the power of optimism and hope in shaping our experiences and outcomes. This card encourages us to cultivate a positive outlook, even in the face of adversity or uncertainty. By maintaining a hopeful attitude, we can tap into our resilience and strength to overcome obstacles and manifest our dreams.

Resilience and Adaptability: Attitude is also about resilience and adaptability, the ability to bounce back from setbacks and adapt to changing circumstances with grace and flexibility. This card reminds us that while we may not always have control over external events, we always have control over our attitude and response.

By cultivating a resilient attitude, we can navigate life's ups and downs with greater ease and confidence.

Gratitude and Appreciation: Attitude invites us to cultivate an attitude of gratitude and appreciation for the blessings in our lives, no matter how small. This card reminds us that gratitude is a powerful antidote to negativity and a key to unlocking greater abundance and joy. By focusing on the things we are grateful for, we shift our perspective towards abundance and open ourselves up to receiving even more blessings.

Empowerment and Self-Belief: Attitude is ultimately about empowerment and self-belief, the confidence and belief in ourselves to create the life we desire. This card encourages us to adopt a mindset of self-empowerment, recognizing our inherent worth and potential to achieve our goals. By cultivating a positive attitude and believing in ourselves, we unlock the door to infinite possibilities and create the life of our dreams.

Takeaway:

Consider cultivating a positive mindset and outlook. Embrace optimism, resilience, and gratitude, knowing that your attitude can shape your experiences and outcomes. Embrace the power of attitude, and watch as you transform challenges into opportunities and dreams into reality with grace and determination.

Exercise:

Attitude Affirmation

"I embrace each day positively, transforming every challenge into a stepping stone for growth and success. When I am not at my most positive, I treat myself with love and compassion and remind myself that I can turn negatives into positives."

AWARENESS

The Awareness card represents being conscious and fully present, deeply attuned to both the inner and outer worlds. It symbolizes heightened perception, mindfulness, and the ability to see things clearly and truthfully. This card invites you to cultivate a deeper awareness of your thoughts, emotions, and surroundings, encouraging you to live with intention and clarity.

Key Meanings:

Heightened Perception: Sharpen your senses and be fully present in your experiences. By paying close attention to your surroundings and your inner state, you can gain valuable insights and respond more effectively to life's challenges.

Mindfulness: This means being fully engaged and present in each moment. Cultivating mindfulness through practices such as meditation, deep breathing, or simply pausing to notice the details of your environment helps you stay grounded and connected.

Clarity and Insight: See situations and people as they truly are without distorted biases or preconceptions. Clear awareness allows you to make more informed and wise decisions.

Living with Intention: Align your actions with your values and be conscious of the choices you make. By living intentionally, you create a more meaningful and fulfilling life.

Takeaway:

Sharpen your perception, practice mindfulness, and seek clarity in your thoughts and actions. Consider how you can enhance your awareness through mindfulness practices, paying close attention to your surroundings and your inner state. By doing so, you can gain valuable insights, make more informed decisions, and live a more intentional
and fulfilling life.

Exercise:

Go with the Flow

Taking things easy is not always easy, but you can get a lot more happiness out of life–in your work and play and in all your relationships–when you lighten up a little. This technique will help you start strong by learning to go with the flow.

I love swimming in the waves at the beach, but near my house, dangerous riptides (strong currents caused by tidal flow) sometimes suck swimmers out into deep water. Now, most people's instinct when caught in a riptide is to fight against it. But that just exhausts you and makes it harder to escape.

Instead of advising to fight against it, did you know that lifeguards teach swimmers to do just the opposite? When caught in a riptide, they say to just "go with the flow"–that is, just swim along with it. Soon, you'll come out of it with no trouble.

The same goes for the inner riptide called stress: If you feel stressed out, tense, uptight, nervous–anything at all–simply dive into your stress,
become aware of it, and you'll find you quickly come out of it.

If you let yourself go with the feeling, experience it, and even exaggerate it, an exciting thing happens. In minutes, the stress just vanishes.
You'll feel energized, not exhausted, because you weren't fighting to get rid of the stress. Instead, you allowed the stress to sweep you along, and quickly, the stress just weakened and disappeared. Perhaps you'll hardly remember what it was. Soon, you'll be peacefully going about your day.

When you have enough awareness to experience stress and give up control, you gain even greater power. Try this the next time you feel a stress riptide trying to pull your mind into a whirlwind of worry.

Go with the Flow in 5 Easy Steps

1. Become aware of your stress.
2. Stop fighting or trying to control it.
3. Feel it. Even exaggerate it!
4. Notice the stress ease up in minutes.
5. Become aware of your new state of mind.

BAGGAGE

The Baggage card symbolizes our burdens from past experiences, relationships, and traumas. It embodies the weight of unresolved emotions, limiting beliefs, and negative patterns we carry on our journey through life. This card invites us to acknowledge and release the baggage that weighs us down, freeing ourselves from the past and reclaiming our power to create a brighter, more fulfilling future.

Key Meanings:

Unresolved Emotions: Baggage represents the emotional wounds and unresolved issues from our past that continue to impact us in the present. This card encourages us to acknowledge and process our emotions, allowing us to feel and express them healthily. By addressing our emotional baggage with compassion and courage, we can release its hold on us and experience greater freedom and healing.

Limiting Beliefs: Baggage also symbolizes the limiting beliefs and negative self-talk that we carry with us, holding us back from realizing our full potential. This card invites us to examine the beliefs and stories we tell ourselves about who we are and what we are capable of and to challenge those that no longer serve us. By releasing limiting beliefs and embracing a mindset of self-love and empowerment, we can transform our lives and manifest our deepest desires.

Patterns and Habits: Baggage may manifest as repetitive patterns and habits that keep us stuck in cycles of self-sabotage and dysfunction. This card reminds us to examine how we may be repeating destructive patterns from our past, whether in relationships, careers, or personal behavior. By bringing awareness to these patterns and making conscious choices to break free from them, we can create space for new, more positive experiences to enter our lives.

Forgiveness and Release: Baggage ultimately calls us to practice forgiveness and release, both for ourselves and others. This card invites us to let go of resentment, anger, and blame towards ourselves and those who have hurt us, recognizing that grudges only perpetuate our suffering. By practicing forgiveness and compassion, we liberate ourselves from the grip of the past
and open ourselves up to the infinite possibilities of the present moment.

Takeaways:

This card is a powerful reminder to confront and release the emotional baggage that weighs us down. It invites us to embark on a journey of healing and self-discovery, freeing ourselves from the burdens of the past and reclaiming our power to create a brighter, more fulfilling future.
Embrace the process of letting go, and watch as you step into a new chapter of your life with renewed lightness, clarity, and joy.

Exercise:

Big, Red Hot Air Balloon

This is one of my all-time favorite techniques for releasing stress and baggage. Right now (and as often as you'd like), picture yourself walking in a beautiful grassy field. The sun is warm, a cool breeze is blowing, and birds float in the bright blue sky. You notice that sitting in the field is a giant red hot-air balloon you can ride in. Curious, you walk over. As you get near it, you have a fantastic idea: To put all your worry, guilt, anger, fear–all your hidden feelings–into the big wicker basket under the balloon. You fill it up, and as you do, you feel lighter.

Then, you cut the ropes holding the hot-air balloon to the ground. As you cut the ropes, one by one, you sever the ties to all that stress. You feel even freer, less connected to it all. And as the balloon lifts off the ground, you still feel happier–it feels so good to see all that pressure and worry floating away!

The higher it soars, the happier and freer you feel. There goes your stress and tension as the balloon keeps drifting higher past the clouds. Pretty soon, it's just a tiny red dot in the sky. And then it's gone. Vanished.

Say goodbye to your stressful issues, thoughts, and feelings–everything you've been carrying around inside.

The Big Red Hot-Air Balloon in 5 Easy Steps

1. Picture yourself walking in a big, grassy field on a beautiful day.
2. Notice the big red hot-air balloon.
3. Put all your hidden feelings in the basket, noticing how you feel as you load them.
4. Cut the ropes holding down the hot-air balloon filled with your stress.
5. Feel the freedom and happiness as your stress floats away into the sky.

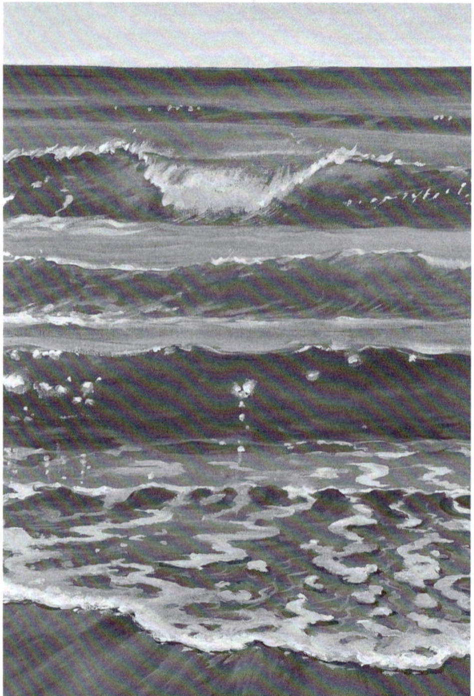

BEING (PRESENT)

The Being (Present) card represents the essence of pure existence, timeless presence. It embodies the state of being fully present in the here and now, free from the constraints of past regrets or future anxieties. This card invites us to connect with the spaciousness and stillness of our inner being, where we can experience a profound sense of peace, clarity, and aliveness.

Key Meanings:

Presence and Awareness: Being (Present) invites us to cultivate awareness by bringing our attention to the present moment and fully inhabiting our experience. This card reminds us that life unfolds in the present moment and that by anchoring ourselves in the here and now, we can experience a profound sense of aliveness and connection to the world around us. By cultivating presence, we awaken to the richness and beauty of life unfolding in
each moment.

Inner Peace and Stillness: Being (Present) is a source of inner peace and stillness, offering us a sanctuary of tranquility amidst the busyness and chaos of everyday life. This card encourages us to cultivate moments of stillness and quietude, whether through meditation, mindfulness, or simply pausing to breathe and center ourselves. By quieting the mind and connecting with the stillness within, we tap into peace and serenity that nourishes our souls and rejuvenates our spirits.

Acceptance and Surrender: Being (Present) invites us to practice acceptance and surrender to the flow of life, embracing each moment exactly as it is, without resistance or judgment. This card reminds us that true peace and freedom lie in surrendering to the present moment, letting go of the need to control or manipulate outcomes, and trusting in the universe's wisdom. By surrendering to what is, we open ourselves to the infinite possibilities and blessings that await us each moment.

Connection to Essence: Being or Presence represents our connection to the essence of who we are–the timeless presence that resides at the core of our being. This card encourages us to peel back the layers of conditioning and identification that obscure our true nature and connect with our soul's radiant essence. By aligning ourselves with our inner being, we awaken to the boundless love, wisdom, and creativity that resides within us and experience a profound sense of wholeness and completeness.

Takeaway:

This card is an invitation to connect with the spaciousness and stillness of your inner being. Cultivate presence and awareness in your life, and embrace each moment with acceptance and surrender. Embrace the wisdom of your inner being, and watch as you awaken to a deeper sense of peace, clarity,
and aliveness.

Exercise:

Extra-Sensory

To enjoy full presence and being, tune into your extra senses!

First, take a couple of deep, satisfying breaths. Then use your imagination to move into your favorite place. Now, let yourself feel your sixth sense, your intuition. What's your intuition feeling right now about taking this time for yourself? What's your heart saying about tuning into your senses?

Be your intuition.

And what's your seventh sense saying about your journey? That's your sense of humor, the lightness and amusement you have to be able to laugh at yourself.
You have to admit there's a silly side to things, and if you ever want to let go, just *be your lighter, humorous self.*

Finally, connect with your eighth sense, your sense of adventure. Let yourself go for it and explore your favorite place. Your sense of adventure will help you break out of your old habits of mind and discover new paths to relaxation.

So, anytime you need to let go of stress, just take a moment to visit this place.
Focus on one sense or use all eight senses: You can see it, feel it, listen, smell, taste, enjoy your intuition, laugh, and explore. This is a place of power, a place free of tension. And once you're in this place for a few moments or a few minutes, you're giving yourself a gift of presence and being.

Extra-Sensory in 6 Easy Steps

1. Take a few deep, satisfying breaths.
2. Move into your favorite place.
3. Be your intuition.
4. Be your sense of humor, light and amused.
5. Be your sense of adventure.
6. Practice enjoying your senses one at a time or all at once in your favorite place.

BREATHE

Breathe is a gentle reminder to return to the present moment, to find solace and strength in simply breathing. This card embodies the essence of mindfulness and presence, inviting us to pause, take a deep breath, and reconnect with the rhythm of our breath. It reminds us that amidst the chaos and busyness of life, the breath serves as a reliable anchor, guiding us back to a state of calmness, clarity, and inner peace.

Key Meanings:

Presence and Awareness: Breathe invites us to cultivate presence and awareness in our lives by anchoring our attention to the present moment through the rhythm of our breath. This card encourages us to let go of worries about the past or anxieties about the future and to simply be here now, fully engaged in the present moment. By bringing our awareness to the breath, we cultivate mindfulness and deepen our connection to the richness and beauty of life unfolding in each moment.

Relaxation and Stress Relief: Breathe is a powerful tool for relaxation and stress relief, offering a sanctuary of peace and calm amidst the demands of everyday life. This card reminds us of the healing power of the breath to soothe the nervous system, quiet the mind, and promote a sense of well-being. By taking slow, deep breaths, we activate the body's relaxation response, reducing stress, anxiety, and tension and restoring mind, body, and spirit balance.

Centering and Grounding: Breathe helps us center and ground ourselves by connecting us to our breath's steady, rhythmic flow. This card encourages us to use the breath as an anchor to navigate the ups and downs of life with grace and resilience. By tuning into the sensation of the breath moving in and out of the body, we anchor ourselves in the present moment, finding stability and strength amidst the ebb and flow of life's challenges.

Renewal and Vitality: Breathe is a source of renewal and vitality, infusing our bodies with life-giving oxygen and revitalizing our energy and spirit. This card reminds us of the power of the breath to replenish and rejuvenate us, filling us with a sense of aliveness and vitality. By taking conscious, intentional breaths, we nourish ourselves at the deepest level, awakening to the inherent beauty and vitality of our being.

Takeaway:

Pause, take a deep breath, and reconnect with the present moment. Embrace the healing power of the breath, finding solace and strength in its rhythmic flow. Embrace the practice of mindful breathing, and watch as you cultivate greater presence, peace, and vitality in your life.

Exercise:

Turning Points

For the next few breaths while you read, focus on your breathing, on the rhythm of your breathing, and the rise and fall of each breath. Remember: how you're breathing is not important. Deep or shallow, nose or mouth, rough or smooth–it really doesn't matter. Simply notice your breathing – inhale, exhale; inhale, exhale – and accept it as it is.

After a few breaths, to take this even deeper, notice the brief pause between exhale and inhale. These are your turning points, and they're in every breath you'll ever take and have ever taken. They last about a millisecond unless you hold your breath.

For this exercise, just observe these turning points without trying to change them. Notice when they come, how long they last, and when they begin to turn. Inhale-*turn*, exhale-*turn*; inhale-*turn*, exhale-*turn*. If you're very quiet and very attentive, you might even notice that there's the tiniest space in the middle of each turning point, a split-second moment of silence poised between the inhale and the exhale.

Observing your turning points reveals something extraordinary, something very grand and straightforward at the same time. Your mind calms, your body relaxes, your hurry and busyness slow down, and you feel peace with yourself.

Turning Points in 4 Easy Steps

1. Follow steps 1 - 5 of Letting Go.
2. Notice your Turning Points when the inhale turns into an exhale and vice versa.
3. Observe your Turning Points and the quiet space between them.
4. Feel your shift towards calmness and self-acceptance.

CATASTROPHIZE

Catastrophizing is the tendency to imagine the worst-case scenario, magnifying potential problems or setbacks to extreme proportions in our minds. This card embodies the essence of catastrophizing, reminding us of our thoughts' power to shape our perceptions and experiences. It invites us to recognize when we engage
in catastrophic thinking and cultivate mindfulness and resilience in uncertainty
and challenges.

Key Meanings:

Magnification of Problems: Catastrophizing involves magnifying problems or setbacks to extreme proportions, imagining the worst possible outcome in any given situation. This card reminds us to be mindful of our tendency to catastrophize, recognizing when our thoughts are spiraling into negativity and fear. By bringing awareness to our catastrophic thinking patterns, we can begin to challenge them
and shift our perspective towards a more balanced and realistic view of reality.

Heightened Anxiety and Stress: Catastrophizing often leads to heightened anxiety and stress as we become overwhelmed by the imagined threats and dangers looming in our minds. This card invites us to cultivate practices that promote relaxation and calmness, such as deep breathing, mindfulness meditation, or physical exercise. By soothing our nervous system and calming our minds, we can reduce the impact of catastrophic thinking on our mental and emotional well-being.

Distorted Perception of Reality: Catastrophizing distorts our perception of reality, causing us to focus exclusively on the negative aspects of a situation while overlooking potential solutions or positive outcomes. This card encourages us to challenge our catastrophic thoughts by asking ourselves whether our fears are based on reality or simply products of our imagination. By reframing our perspective and focusing on solutions rather than problems, we can regain control and empowerment in adversity.

Cultivation of Resilience: Catastrophizing presents an opportunity for growth and resilience as we learn to navigate the challenges and uncertainties of life with greater courage and strength. This card reminds us that we have the power to choose how we respond to difficult situations and that we can cultivate resilience by adopting a more balanced and optimistic mindset. By reframing catastrophic thoughts as opportunities for growth and learning, we can build resilience and fortitude in adversity.

Takeaway:

Remember that your thoughts have a big impact on your perceptions and experiences. Recognize when you are engaging in catastrophic thinking and cultivate resilience and perspective in the face of uncertainty and challenges. Embrace the opportunity for growth and resilience, and watch as you develop the inner strength and courage to navigate life's ups and downs with grace and resilience.

Exercise:

Recognize when you are catastrophizing: pause and take a few deep breaths when you notice yourself imagining the worst-case scenario. Write down the situation and list the most likely, realistic outcomes alongside your catastrophic thoughts. Reflect on how often the worst-case scenario actually happens, and practice reframing your thoughts to focus on manageable and constructive solutions.

CHANGE

Change is the constant companion on life's journey, guiding us through the ebb and flow of transformation and growth. This card embodies the essence of evolution, adaptation, and renewal, reminding us that change is an inevitable and natural part of the human experience. It invites us to embrace the opportunities for growth and transformation that change brings, trusting in the universe's wisdom to guide us through times of transition.

Key Meanings:

Transformation and Growth: Change is a catalyst for transformation and growth, inviting us to shed old ways of being and embrace new possibilities. This card encourages us to embrace change as an opportunity for personal evolution and self-discovery, trusting in the process of growth and renewal that unfolds with each new chapter of our lives.

Adaptation and Resilience: Change often brings challenges and uncertainties, testing our ability to adapt and respond with resilience. This card reminds us of our innate capacity to navigate change with grace and strength, trusting in our inner resources and wisdom to guide us through times of transition. By cultivating flexibility and resilience, we empower ourselves to weather life's storms and emerge stronger and wiser on the other side.

Embracing the Unknown: Change can be unsettling and uncomfortable, stirring up feelings of fear, doubt, and uncertainty. This card encourages us to embrace the unknown with courage and openness, trusting in the inherent wisdom and guidance of the universe to lead us forward. By surrendering to the flow of change and releasing our attachment to outcomes, we create space for new possibilities to emerge and unfold.

Embracing Impermanence: Change reminds us of the impermanent nature of all things, inviting us to let go of attachments and embrace the transient beauty of the present moment. This card encourages us to embrace impermanence as a natural and essential aspect of life, honoring the cycles of birth, growth, death, and rebirth that shape our existence. By embracing change with acceptance and gratitude, we deepen our appreciation for life's fleeting beauty and preciousness.

Takeaway:

This card is a reminder to embrace the inevitable flow of change with courage, resilience, and openness. It encourages us to see change as an opportunity for growth, transformation, and renewal, trusting in the universe's wisdom to guide us through times of transition. Embrace the spirit of change, and watch your journey unfold with new possibilities, insights, and opportunities for growth and evolution.

Exercise:

Slow Down

Change takes time, and that's okay!

Imagine a giant redwood tree. They take hundreds of years to grow over 350 feet tall. Once they do, they're resilient and strong, unlike the delicate seasonal flower that comes and goes in a few weeks. Be a redwood tree and see your growth as consistent and deep-rooted. Slow down and take your time. You deserve it.

Enjoy and celebrate every step, and let go of any judgment and criticism you may have about your pace. Rushing will likely only produce temporary results.

Your path may not be perfect, but at least you're on it! When you rush, you miss the stars, the trees, the joy, wins, and all the beauty in your life.

Allow yourself the gift of experiencing life's journey of change and evolution and all it offers. Acknowledge and celebrate your growth, no matter how big or small

Slow Down in 3 Easy Steps

1. Imagine yourself as a redwood tree; resilient, strong, and deep-rooted.
2. Slow down, acknowledge, and celebrate your inner growth.
3. Repeat as often as necessary with self-love and grace.

COMMITTEE MEETING

The Committee Meeting card symbolizes the committee gathering of emotions that we all have within us. It reminds us that every emotion has a seat at the table and deserves to be acknowledged, heard, and respected. This card invites us to hold a committee meeting that includes all of our emotions, so we can hear the wisdom that is innately imparted by each, even if that wisdom is empathizing with and recognizing the history and origins of a tumultuous committee meeting.

Key Meanings:

Repressed Emotions: The Committee Meeting is an invitation to all emotions, where each an has a seat at the table and has the opportunity to be heard. This includes the emotions typically labeled "bad," that we tend to avoid or repress. When you allow challenging emotions like frustration, anger, sadness, or shame to take a stand and speak up, you have the opportunity to listen carefully and understand where it's coming from and why it's presented itself, oftentimes in an act of self-preservation due to past experiences.

Conducting a Committee Meeting: When you conduct a Committee Meeting, imagine a conference table where every emotion has a seat. Happy, sad, mad, frustrated, hopeful, helpless–all are welcome. Then, give each feeling an opportunity to share what they feel and why. No interruptions–just listening with friendliness, care, and compassion.

Moving Forward with Your Committee: Once each Committee Member has had a turn to speak, you'll notice that you feel much more relaxed immediately. You'll be able to take what you learned from each committee member and act accordingly, considering what is valid and gently moving past any reactive sentiments that don't serve you.

Takeaways:

The Committee Meeting is the gathering of emotions that we all have within us where every emotion has a seat at the table and deserves to be acknowledged, heard, and respected. Give voice to every emotion, including the challenging ones, and consider that there is wisdom and learning in each. Conduct a Committee Meeting regularly to learn from each committee member, considering what is valid and what doesn't serve you. By giving each emotion a voice, you'll experience a feeling of inner peace and lightness that will allow your future Committee Meetings to be even more productive and impactful.

Exercise:

Conduct a Committee Meeting

Conduct a Committee Meeting using the instructions above.
What emotions showed up, and what did they say?
What do you notice about yourself emotionally after conducting the Committee Meeting?

COMPASSION

Compassion is the gentle touch of understanding, the warm embrace of empathy, and the boundless wellspring of kindness that flows from the heart. This card embodies the essence of love, empathy, and altruism, reminding us of the transformative power of compassion in healing wounds, bridging divides, and fostering connection. It invites us to cultivate compassion towards ourselves and others, recognizing the inherent worth and dignity of every being.

Key Meanings:

Empathy and Understanding: Compassion begins with the ability to empathize with the experiences and emotions of others, recognizing their joys, sorrows, and struggles as our own. This card encourages us to cultivate a compassionate heart, listening deeply to the stories and feelings of those around us with openness and empathy. By extending understanding and acceptance to others, we create a safe space for healing and connection.

Kindness and Generosity: Compassion inspires acts of kindness and generosity towards others, offering support, assistance, and comfort to those in need. This card reminds us of the power of small gestures to make a big difference in someone's life–a smile, a kind word, a helping hand. By practicing random acts of kindness and compassion, we create ripples of love and positivity that uplift others and ourselves.

Self-Compassion and Forgiveness: Compassion begins within ourselves as we learn to extend the same kindness, understanding, and forgiveness to ourselves

that we offer to others. This card invites us to cultivate self-compassion by embracing our imperfections, honoring our needs, and treating ourselves with gentleness and care.
By practicing self-compassion and forgiveness, we heal our wounds and create space for greater love and acceptance to flourish within us.

Connection and Unity: Compassion is a powerful force that unites us in our shared humanity, transcending differences of race, religion, or background. This card encourages us to recognize the inherent worth and dignity of every being and extend compassion and respect to all living beings. By fostering a sense of connection and unity with others, we create a more compassionate and inclusive world for all.

Takeaway:

This card reminds you to open your heart to the suffering and joys of the world with compassion and empathy. It encourages you to practice kindness, generosity, and forgiveness toward yourself and others, recognizing the transformative power of love to heal, unite, and uplift. Embrace the spirit of compassion, and watch as your world becomes infused with greater love, understanding, and connection.

Exercise:

See Yourself Better

When you see how beautiful and wonderful your body is, you'll pay attention to its needs, its signals, and what it wants. When your body tells you something, you'll listen to it and trust it. And when you practice self-compassion, it becomes much easier to extend compassion toward others.

A way to open up this channel of communication is by slowly and gently saying these three lines directly to your body:

1.) "Thank you for working so well for me all these years."

2.) "I'm sorry if I've been ignoring you."

3.) "If there's anything you're trying to tell me, I'm open right now."

Repeat these lines, speaking aloud and bringing all your attention to your body.

Take a few moments daily and let your body know you're ready to listen. Then, *listen*. The answers you'll get from inside yourself are amazing. The best thing about this new relationship with your body is that it's reciprocal; the more you love and take care of your body, the more it will love and take care of you.

Talk to your body–and listen to it–to become more compassionate to yourself and others.

See Yourself Better in 5 Easy Steps

1. Take a deep belly breath and bring your attention to your body.
2. Slowly say these three lines to your body:
   - "Thank you for working so well for me all these years."
   - "I'm sorry if I've been ignoring you."
   - "If there's anything you're trying to tell me, I'm open right now."
3. Remain quiet, noting any shifts, changes, or sensations in your body.
4. Repeat steps two and three.
5. Reflect on any communications you've received from inside yourself.

CONNECTION

Connection is the invisible thread that binds us, weaving a tapestry of relationships that nourish, support, and enrich our lives. This card embodies the essence of unity, belonging, and interdependence, reminding us of the profound connections that link us to one another and to the web of life itself. It invites us to cultivate deeper connections with ourselves, others, and the world around us, recognizing the inherent beauty and significance of our interconnectedness.

Key Meanings:

Relationships and Community: Connection is at the heart of our relationships with others, forming the foundation of community, friendship, and love. This card encourages us to cultivate deeper connections with the people in our lives, fostering bonds of trust, empathy, and mutual support. By nurturing meaningful relationships

and fostering a sense of belonging, we create a support network that sustains us through life's ups and downs.

Self-Reflection and Inner Connection: Connection begins within ourselves as we cultivate a deeper relationship with our innermost thoughts, feelings, and desires. This card invites us to practice self-reflection and introspection, exploring the depths of our inner world with curiosity and compassion. By nurturing a sense of inner connection and self-awareness, we gain clarity, resilience, and a deeper understanding of ourselves and our place in the world.

Nature and the Cosmos: Connection extends beyond our relationships with others to include our connection with the natural world and the universe. This card reminds us of our interconnectedness with all living beings and the earth itself, inviting us to honor and respect the web of life that sustains us. By cultivating a sense of reverence and gratitude for nature, we deepen our connection to the earth and foster a sense of stewardship and responsibility for its well-being.

Spiritual Connection: Connection is also a spiritual concept, representing our connection to something greater than ourselves–a higher power, universal consciousness, or divine source of love and wisdom. This card encourages us to nurture our spiritual connection through meditation, prayer, or mindfulness. By cultivating a sense of reverence and awe for the mystery and wonder of existence, we tap into a wellspring of inspiration, guidance, and inner peace.

Takeaway:

Interdependence and unity that underlies all of existence. Nurture a deeper connection with yourself, others, and the world around you, recognizing the beauty and significance of all interconnectedness. Embrace the spirit of connection, and watch as your relationships deepen, your sense of belonging expands, and your heart opens to the boundless love and wisdom that flows through the web of life.

Exercise:

Tree Roots

Right now, put your feet flat on the ground wherever you're sitting. Change positions if you have to, but get both feet flat. As you do this, give all your attention to the feelings in your feet, your heels, the balls of your feet, and your toes. As you focus on your feet, you may notice some interesting sensations, like heaviness or tingling.

Now, with your feet flat on the ground, imagine your feet have roots in the earth. Feel the roots coming out of your feet, right through the floor and into the soil underneath; maybe a foot, then two, three, four, five feet. Feel them reaching and spreading out into the earth.

Like a tree, you are now firmly connected to the earth. You are grounded, relaxed, and secure from your roots to the top of your head.

You can do this anytime. Feel, visualize, and experience a beautiful state of inner peace.

Tree Roots in 4 Easy Steps

1. Put your feet flat on the ground and bring your awareness to them.
2. Imagine roots stretching from the bottoms of your feet into the earth.
3. Feel and visualize these roots growing, stretching, and connecting downwards and outwards in the earth.
4. Imagine yourself firmly connected to the earth and grounded in relaxation and peace.

CONSCIOUS (MIND)

The Conscious Mind card represents the power of awareness and intentionality in shaping our thoughts, beliefs, and experiences. It embodies the essence of mindfulness and mental clarity, inviting us to cultivate a deeper connection with our conscious awareness and harness its transformative potential. This card reminds us that by bringing awareness to our thoughts and beliefs, we can unlock the power to shape our reality and create a life aligned with our highest intentions.

Key Meanings:

Mindfulness and Presence: The conscious mind invites us to cultivate mindfulness and presence in our daily lives by bringing our attention to the present moment and anchoring ourselves in the here and now. This card reminds us that our power lies in the present moment and that by cultivating awareness of our thoughts and experiences, we can access the wisdom and guidance of our conscious mind to navigate life with clarity and intention.

Clarity and Insight: The conscious mind is a source of clarity and insight, offering us a clear lens through which to perceive reality and make informed choices. This card encourages us to cultivate mental clarity by questioning our beliefs, assumptions, and perceptions and seeking a deeper understanding of ourselves and the world around us. By tapping into the wisdom of our conscious mind, we gain insight into the patterns and dynamics that shape our lives, empowering us to make conscious choices that align with our highest values and aspirations.

Empowerment and Transformation: The conscious mind represents the power of conscious awareness to catalyze transformation and growth in our lives. This card reminds us that we can shape our reality through the thoughts we choose to focus on and the beliefs we choose to hold.

By cultivating positive thoughts, affirming beliefs, and aligning our intentions with our actions, we can harness the transformative power

of our conscious mind to create a life filled with meaning, purpose, and fulfillment.

Alignment with Higher Truth: The conscious mind invites us to align our conscious awareness with the higher truth of our soul's journey, recognizing that our true nature is inherently wise, loving, and compassionate. This card encourages us to transcend the egoic mind's limitations and tap into our soul's deeper wisdom, where we find clarity, guidance, and purpose. By aligning our conscious awareness with the higher truth of our soul, we awaken to the boundless potential that resides within us and unlock the keys to living a life of joy, abundance, and spiritual fulfillment.

Takeaway:

When the Conscious (Mind) card appears in a reading, it reminds you to cultivate mindfulness and mental clarity. It invites you to bring conscious awareness to your thoughts, beliefs, and experiences and harness the transformative power of your conscious mind to create a life aligned with your highest intentions. Embrace the wisdom of your conscious mind, and watch as you awaken to new insights, opportunities, and possibilities for growth and transformation.

Exercise:

Enhance your conscious awareness: spend a few minutes daily in mindful observation, paying close attention to your thoughts and surroundings without judgment. Write down any patterns or recurring thoughts, reflecting on how they influence your daily life and decisions. Use this awareness to make intentional choices that align with your

goals and values.

EMOTIONS

Emotions are the vibrant colors that paint the canvas of our inner landscape, expressing the richness and complexity of our human experience. This card delves into the depths of our emotional world, inviting us to explore the myriad feelings that flow through us–joy, sorrow, love, anger, fear, and everything in between. It reminds us that our emotions are a natural and essential part of being human, guiding us toward greater self-awareness, authenticity, and connection with others.

Key Meanings:

Self-Awareness and Reflection: Emotions serve as mirrors that reflect our innermost thoughts, beliefs, and desires. This card encourages us to focus on our emotions and explore their underlying meanings and messages. By becoming more self-aware and reflective of our feelings, we gain deeper insights into ourselves and the experiences that shape our lives.

Acceptance and Expression: Emotions are meant to be felt, acknowledged, and expressed–not suppressed or denied. This card reminds us that it is okay to experience a wide range of emotions, from the highest highs to the lowest lows. By embracing our emotions with acceptance and compassion, we create space for healing, growth, and authentic self-expression.

Navigating Relationships: Emotions play a central role in our relationships with others, shaping the way we connect, communicate, and relate to one another. This card encourages us to be mindful of our emotions in our interactions with others, recognizing how our feelings influence the dynamics of our relationships. We foster deeper connections

and create more fulfilling relationships by cultivating empathy, compassion, and emotional intelligence.

Emotional Balance and Regulation: While emotions are a natural part of being human, it is important to maintain a sense of balance and regulation in our emotional lives. This card reminds us to practice self-care and emotional resilience, find healthy ways to cope with stress, regulate our moods, navigate challenging emotions, and develop emotional awareness and coping skills. Developing these skills empowers us to respond to life's ups and downs with grace and resilience.

Takeaway:

You are invited to dive into the depths of your emotional world and explore the feelings that arise within you. Embrace your emotions with curiosity, compassion, and acceptance, recognizing them as valuable messengers guiding you toward greater self-awareness and connection. By honoring your emotions and learning to navigate them with skill and sensitivity, you can cultivate emotional resilience, deepen your relationships, and live more authentically and fully.

Exercise:

Journaling with Your Non-Dominant Hand

Journal, but with your non-dominant hand! This will allow you the time to better process your emotions.

Let's say you're angry at someone. It could be your boss, your partner, or even yourself. Write down in as much detail as possible how you're feeling physically, for example, "I feel tight in my stomach…my breathing is shallow…my face is tense…" Just write in your non-dominant hand whatever your body is feeling. Then, write your emotions down. For example, "I'm so angry at my boss. Angry, angry, angry! What a jerk!" Blast away, write BIG, stab the paper with your pencil...go for it! Let your anger flow as you write, scribble, or doodle precisely how you're feeling. It would be hard to re-read your non-dominant hand

scribble-scrabble anyway, so hold nothing back.

You can also look back at things from your past that still make you feel ashamed, angry, guilty, or confused. Express whatever and however you'd like using your non-dominant hand. Just spontaneously and freely allow whatever to happen, happen. You may cry. You may doodle and draw. You may journal. Whatever comes out is perfect.

Get in the habit of describing the feelings at the root of your stress and writing them with your non-dominant hand. Afterward, how do you feel? Relieved? Have your feelings lost some of their charge? This is a very effective strategy for becoming aware of your stress, expressing it, and then reducing it in a healthy and effective way.

Non-Dominant Hand Journaling in 6 Easy Steps

1. Get paper or a journal and a pencil.
2. With your non-dominant hand, write your physical feelings.
3. With your non-dominant hand, write your internal feelings–your emotions.
4. Describe your stress in whatever way feels best.
5. Let your emotions flow through your writing.
6. Take a moment to become aware of how your feelings have evolved throughout this exercise.

FANTASY

Fantasy is the enchanted realm of imagination where dreams take flight and possibilities are limitless. This card invites us to explore the magical landscape of our inner world, where fantasies and dreams hold sway over reality. It reminds us that the seeds of creativity, inspiration, and boundless potential lie within our imagination.

Key Meanings:

Exploration of Imagination: Fantasy encourages us to journey into the depths of our imagination, where anything is possible. This card invites us to unleash our creativity and embrace the wonders of the fantastical realm within us. By allowing our minds to wander freely and explore new ideas, we expand our horizons and cultivate a sense of wonder and curiosity that enriches our lives.

Escape and Release: Fantasy can serve as a temporary escape from the trials and tribulations of everyday life. This card reminds us that it is okay to retreat into the realm of fantasy occasionally, allowing ourselves to dream, play, and indulge in flights of fancy. By releasing ourselves from the constraints of reality, even briefly,
we rejuvenate our spirits and replenish our creative energies.

Inspiration and Creativity: Fantasy is a wellspring of inspiration and creativity, offering endless possibilities for artistic expression and innovation. This card encourages us to draw upon the fantastical realm of our imagination as a source of inspiration for our creative endeavors. Whether through art, writing, music, or any other form of self-expression, we can tap into the magic of fantasy to bring our visions to life in wondrous and unexpected ways.

Balance and Grounding: While fantasy can be a source of joy and inspiration, it is important to maintain a sense of balance and grounding in our lives. This card reminds us not to lose ourselves entirely in fantasy but to remain rooted in reality and connected to the present moment. By finding harmony between our dreams and responsibilities, we can harness the power of fantasy to enrich our lives without losing touch with the world around us.

Takeaway:

This card encourages you to embrace the magic of imagination and creativity. It invites you to explore the fantastical realm within you,
where dreams take flight and possibilities are limitless. By tapping into the power of fantasy, you can ignite your creativity, find inspiration,
and infuse your life with wonder and enchantment. Embrace the magic of fantasy, and watch as your world expands with endless possibilities and boundless joy.

Exercise:

Take a moment to fantasize! If there were no limits or boundaries, what would you create? What would you do? What would you experience? When anything is possible, what are you drawn to? Journal about this, and be as specific and detailed as possible.

FEAR

Fear is the shadow that looms over the landscape of our psyche, casting doubt, uncertainty, and anxiety upon our path. This card delves into the depths of our fears, exploring how they shape our thoughts, beliefs, and behaviors. It reminds us that while fear is a natural and instinctual response to perceived threats, it can also become a barrier that holds us back from realizing our true potential and living life to the fullest.

Key Meanings:

Awareness and Acknowledgment: Fear thrives in the shadows of our subconscious mind, often exerting its influence over our thoughts and actions without conscious awareness. This card encourages us to shine a light on our fears, bringing them into the open so we can acknowledge and confront them directly. By facing our fears with courage and honesty, we reclaim our power and diminish their hold over us.

Understanding Root Causes: Fear can stem from various sources, including past traumas, limiting beliefs, and perceived threats to our safety or security. This card invites us to explore the root causes of our fears, uncovering the underlying patterns and triggers that fuel our anxiety and apprehension. By gaining insight into our fears' origins, we can dismantle their hold on our psyche and cultivate greater emotional resilience.

Embracing Courage: Courage is not the absence of fear but the willingness to confront it head-on and move forward despite it.
This card reminds us that we have within us the strength and resilience to overcome our fears and pursue our dreams with unwavering determination. By embracing courage and stepping outside our comfort zone, we expand our horizons, unlock new opportunities, and experience personal growth and transformation.

Transformation and Liberation: Fear can be a powerful catalyst for growth and change when we confront it with courage and compassion.
This card encourages us to see our fears as opportunities for self-discovery and liberation rather than obstacles to be avoided or overcome. By embracing the lessons that fear has to teach us and embracing the unknown with an open heart, we can transcend our limitations and emerge stronger, wiser, and more empowered than ever before.

Takeaway:

This card reminds you to acknowledge and confront the fears that keep you from realizing your true potential. It encourages you to embrace courage, self-awareness, and compassion as you navigate life's challenges and uncertainties. By facing your fears with honesty and resilience, you can transform them into sources of strength, wisdom, and liberation, ultimately freeing yourself to live authentically and fearlessly.

Exercise:

Say It 3 Times

Here's an easy way to face your fear: Become aware of your fear and notice that it's inside you. Now, take a deep breath and name it slowly three times.

For example, just notice it, breathe deeply, and say to yourself, "fear...fear...fear." Say it aloud or to yourself. Say it slowly three times.

By saying what you're feeling three times, you become more aware of that feeling and more present with it. And once you become more aware of the emotion, something incredible happens: The feeling loses its power. You separate from it once you're aware, conscious, and focused
on its presence. Soon, you're back in the present, and your stress has melted away.

Say It 3 Times in 3 Easy Steps

1. Identify what you are feeling.
2. Become aware of the feeling.
3. Take a deep breath and name it slowly three times, in your head or aloud.

FIFTEENTH ROW

The Fifteenth Row card symbolizes the inner critic seated in the fifteenth row of the movie theater showing the movie of your life. It brings light to the side of ourselves that is judgmental, critical, and negative and invites us to respect, recognize, and accept this perspective to quiet it and move to the Last Row–where our truest self is seated and watching with friendliness, care, and compassion.

Key Meanings:

Judgment: The Fifteenth Row invites us to look at where we might be looking at ourselves and others with harsh judgment. The inner critic that is seated in the fifteenth row of your inner theater will always be within us, but by giving them a voice, we allow them to be quieted so we can move into a space of self-compassion and love.

Self-Criticism: When we listen to our loud fifteenth-row inner critic, the self-criticism can be deafening. Explore the origins of this self-criticism and face it head-on

for what it is: your inner critic speaking from a place of pain, fear, or trauma. By empathizing with this voice, you can move one step closer to the uplifting and inspiring Last Row higher self.

Negativity: Negativity lives in the fifteenth row. Your inner critic will find negativity in everything, making you doubt yourself and every step you take along the road of life. When you find yourself spiraling into negative thoughts, recognize where you are in the movie theater of your life and take steps to gently make your way back to the Last Row where you will have a healthier and more empowered view of your life, capacity, and decisions.

Takeaway:

Your fifteenth-row inner critic will always be there. By giving them a voice, you allow them to be quieted so you can move into the Last Row, where your true self sits with love, friendliness, care, and compassion. Accept and work with your fifteenth-row inner critic, and discover a life of harmony, self-acceptance, and deep inner peace.

Exercise:

Fly Away

After a couple of deep, satisfying breaths, imagine you're at the airport saying goodbye to your 15th-row Inner Critic. You've decided to send them off on a short vacation.

So, you see them board the plane, find their seats, put on their seatbelts, and settle in. Then the plane taxis and takes off, and as you watch the plane climbing into the sky, you feel that the stress is no longer inside you but up in the silver airplane, flying away into the blue sky.

Soon, you feel like you're a cloud watching the plane–just a cloud floating, watching the plane with these stressful people inside. And then you feel like you're the sky–the blue sky–watching the clouds, watching the plane, watching your stress inside the aircraft as it soars out of sight.

Now, don't imagine they're gone for good. They'll be back before you know it; in fact, you'll probably pick them up at the airport. But by letting go of your stress in this way, and as often as you need to, you'll be more relaxed and friendly toward yourself.

Fly Away in 6 Easy Steps

1. Take a few deep, satisfying breaths.
2. Imagine yourself at the airport saying goodbye to your 15th-row inner critic.
3. Watch their process of boarding, settling in, and taking off.
4. See your stress on that plane and no longer inside of you.
5. Feel like a cloud, then the sky, observing the plane fly out of sight.
6. Recognize these stressors aren't gone for good but don't need to be stressed about right now.

FOCUS

Focus is the guiding light that illuminates the path to clarity, productivity, and achievement. This card embodies the power of concentration, intentionality, and single-minded pursuit of our goals. It reminds us that by directing our energy and attention toward what truly matters, we can overcome distractions, stay on course, and manifest our dreams precisely and purposefully.

Key Meanings:

Clarity of Purpose: Focus begins with clearly understanding our goals, values, and priorities. This card encourages us to clarify our intentions and align our actions with our deepest desires and aspirations. By defining what truly matters to us and staying true to our purpose, we can channel our energy and efforts toward meaningful pursuits that bring us fulfillment and joy.

Concentration and Mindfulness: Focus requires concentrating on the task at hand and maintaining mindfulness in the present moment. This card reminds us to cultivate practices that enhance our concentration, such as meditation, deep breathing, or mindful awareness. By quieting the noise of distraction and honing
our focus, we can tap into our inner reservoir of clarity and wisdom.

Eliminating Distractions: Focus is often challenged by the myriad distractions and demands of modern life. This card encourages us to identify and eliminate anything that pulls us away from our goals and intentions, whether external distractions or internal obstacles like doubt or fear.
By creating a conducive environment for focus and productivity,
we empower ourselves to stay on track and make steady progress towards our

objectives.

Commitment and Persistence: Focus is sustained through commitment and persistence, even when facing challenges and setbacks. This card reminds us to stay resolute in our pursuit of excellence, trust in our abilities, and stay true to our vision, even when the journey becomes difficult. By cultivating a mindset of perseverance and resilience, we can overcome obstacles and achieve success beyond our wildest dreams.

Takeaway:

This card reminds us to harness the power of concentration, intentionality, and single-minded pursuit of our goals. It encourages us to clarify our intentions, eliminate distractions, and stay committed to our path with unwavering determination. By cultivating focus, we can unlock our full potential, achieve our goals, and manifest our dreams with clarity, purpose, and precision.

Exercise:

Balancing Act (Variation)

Whenever you're walking, focus on the weight shift between your right foot and your left foot. Feel present in your walking, as if you fully inhabit each footstep. Within a few steps, you'll feel great energy and strength in your legs and notice how focused you can be on something you do so naturally. You'll feel solid, firm, balanced, and focused. Do this again several times, feeling the shift of power, and then just stop and stand in the middle with your weight evenly distributed.

Learning to focus on a simple task physically and mentally will help you tap into that focus in anything you desire to do.

Balancing Act in 3 Easy Steps

1. Put all your weight on your right foot, then your left foot. Notice how it feels.
2. Walk while maintaining focus on this simple movement.
3. Stand on both feet, centered and balanced.

FREEDOM

Freedom is the soaring eagle that knows no bounds, the boundless expanse of the open sky that beckons us to spread our wings and fly. This card embodies the essence of liberation, empowerment, and self-expression. It reminds us that true freedom is not merely the absence of constraints but the ability to embrace our authenticity, follow our passions, and live on our terms.

Key Meanings:

Self-Expression and Authenticity: Freedom invites us to embrace our true selves and authentically express our unique gifts, passions, and perspectives. This card encourages us to break free from societal expectations, cultural norms, and self-imposed limitations that hinder our ability to live in alignment with our deepest desires and values. By honoring our inner truth and embracing our authenticity,
we liberate ourselves to live with passion, purpose, and joy.

Emotional Liberation: Freedom encompasses the liberation of the heart and soul from the shackles of fear, doubt, and past wounds. This card encourages us to release limiting beliefs, negative patterns, and emotional baggage that weigh us down and hold us back from experiencing true joy and fulfillment. By cultivating self-love, acceptance, and forgiveness, we free ourselves from the chains of the past and open our hearts to the boundless possibilities of the present moment.

Empowerment and Choice: Freedom is the power to choose our path, forge our destiny, and create our desired life. This card reminds us that we always have the power to decide how we respond to life's challenges and opportunities, no matter our circumstances. By embracing our agency and taking ownership of our choices, we reclaim our power and sovereignty, empowering ourselves to create a life of purpose, passion, and fulfillment.

Spiritual Liberation: Freedom extends beyond the physical realm into the realm of the spirit, encompassing a sense of inner peace, wholeness,

and spiritual liberation. This card encourages us to connect with our inner wisdom, intuition, and divine essence, trusting in the inherent guidance and support of the universe. By surrendering to the flow of life and aligning with our purpose, we experience a profound sense of freedom and spiritual fulfillment.

Takeaway:

Herald a period of liberation, empowerment, and self-discovery. This is your invitation to break free from limitations, embrace your authenticity, and live with courage, passion, and purpose. Embrace the spirit of freedom, and watch as your world expands with infinite possibilities, boundless joy, and the exhilarating sense of soaring beyond the confines of ordinary existence.

Exercise:

Everyone has a different perspective on what freedom is to them. In your journal, explore what freedom means to you.

- What are the core values of freedom?
- What does it look and feel like?
- In what ways do you feel free?
- In what ways would you like to feel more freedom?

FRIENDLINESS

Friendliness is a gentle breeze that sweeps through the landscape of our relationships, bringing warmth, kindness, and connection. This card embodies the essence of openness, approachability, and genuine goodwill towards others.
It reminds us of the power of a friendly smile, a listening ear, and a welcoming heart in fostering harmonious connections and uplifting the spirits of those around us.

Key Meanings:

Warmth and Hospitality: Friendliness invites us to create a welcoming and inviting atmosphere in our interactions. This card encourages us to greet each person we encounter with warmth, kindness, and genuine interest, making them feel valued, respected, and accepted. By cultivating an atmosphere of hospitality, we create space for meaningful connections to flourish.

Approachability and Openness: Friendliness invites us to be open and approachable. This card reminds us to let down our guard, drop our defenses, and approach each encounter openly and curiously. By embracing the diversity of human experience and welcoming others into our lives with open arms, we create opportunities for connection and understanding to blossom.

Empathy and Compassion: Friendliness is grounded in empathy and compassion for the experiences and feelings of others. This card encourages us to listen attentively, offer support, and extend a helping hand to those in need. By showing genuine concern and understanding for the struggles and joys of others, we cultivate deeper connections and foster a sense of belonging and community.

Harmonious Relationships: Friendliness plays a key role in nurturing harmonious relationships and fostering a sense of unity and cooperation among individuals. This card encourages us to approach conflicts with empathy, patience, and a willingness to find common ground. By practicing forgiveness, understanding, and reconciliation, we can overcome differences and build bridges of friendship that withstand the test of time.

Takeaway:

This card gently reminds you to infuse your interactions with warmth, kindness, and goodwill towards others. Feel invited to cultivate an atmosphere of hospitality, approachability, and inclusivity in your relationships, creating space for meaningful connections to flourish. Embrace the spirit of friendliness, and watch as your world becomes enriched with laughter, understanding, and the joy of authentic connection.

Exercise:

As you go about your day today, make it a point to be friendly. Whether on the road, with your local barista, or with a fellow passerby on the street, make conversation, lend a helping hand, or simply make eye contact, acknowledge them, and smile. See how far friendliness can take you and how good it feels to connect in this way.

GENEROSITY

Generosity is a radiant beacon of light that illuminates the path of kindness, compassion, and abundance. This card embodies the spirit of giving freely and abundantly through generosity, compassion, or heartfelt presence. It reminds us
that true wealth lies not in what we possess but in what we willingly share with others.

Key Meanings:

Open-Hearted Giving: Generosity expresses an open heart and a generous spirit. This card encourages us to freely give our time, resources, and talents without expectation of reward or recognition. By helping others and sharing our blessings with the world, we cultivate a sense of abundance and interconnectedness that enriches both the giver and the receiver.

Gratitude and Appreciation: Generosity springs from a deep well of gratitude and appreciation for the blessings in our lives. When we recognize the abundance that surrounds us and acknowledge the gifts we have received, we naturally feel compelled to share our abundance with others. This card reminds us to cultivate an attitude of gratitude and to express our appreciation through acts of generosity
and kindness.

Spiritual Fulfillment: Generosity is not just about giving material gifts
but also about offering our presence, attention, and love to others. This card encourages us to be generous with our time, listening ear,
and compassionate presence, as these gifts can bring profound comfort, healing, and connection to those in need. By sharing our light with others, we contribute to the greater good and find deep fulfillment in service to others.

Abundance Consciousness: Generosity is rooted in the belief that there is more than enough to go around–that abundance is not a finite resource but an infinite wellspring that flows abundantly for all. This card invites us to cultivate an abundance consciousness, releasing any scarcity mindset or fear of lack and trusting in the inherent abundance of the universe. When we give freely from a place of abundance, we invite even greater blessings into our lives.

Takeaway:

You are invited to remember the profound power of giving and sharing. Open our hearts and hands to others, freely offering your time, resources, and love. Through acts of generosity, you enrich the lives of those around you and nurture a deep sense of fulfillment, connection, and abundance within yourself. Embrace the spirit of generosity, and watch your world expand with love, joy, and infinite blessings.

Exercise:

Generosity Practice

How can you be generous today? Generosity comes in all shapes and sizes, and it's the thought and intention that counts. Can you be generous with your compliments? Can you be in service to someone today? Can you be generous with your time or money?

Do something generous today!

GUILT

Guilt is a powerful and complex emotion that arises from a sense of wrongdoing or moral transgression. This card delves into the depths of our conscience, exploring how guilt can impact our thoughts, emotions, and actions. While often uncomfortable, guilt can serve as a valuable signal, guiding us toward introspection, accountability, and healing.

Key Meanings:

Conscience and Morality: Guilt arises from our internal moral compass, signaling when we have acted in a way that contradicts our values or beliefs. This card encourages us to listen to the whispers of our conscience and take responsibility for our actions, even when it is uncomfortable to do so. By acknowledging our mistakes and their impact on others, we can begin the process of healing and reconciliation.

Self-Reflection and Growth: Guilt invites us to deeply self-reflect, examining the motivations behind our actions and the consequences they have caused. It catalyzes personal growth, prompting us to learn from our mistakes and strive to become better versions of ourselves. This card reminds us that guilt may be painful but can also be transformative, leading to greater self-awareness and empathy.

Forgiveness and Redemption: While guilt can be a powerful force, it is not meant to be a permanent state of being. This card encourages us to seek forgiveness from others and ourselves as an essential step in healing. By acknowledging our mistakes, making amends where possible, and committing to positive change, we can release the grip of guilt and move forward with a renewed sense of purpose and integrity.

Release and Liberation: Ultimately, the guilt journey is one of release and liberation. This card reminds us that we are not defined by our past actions or mistakes. Through self-forgiveness and acceptance, we can unburden ourselves from guilt and reclaim our sense of worthiness and dignity. By embracing our humanity, with all its flaws and imperfections, we can find freedom from the chains of guilt and embrace a life of greater authenticity and compassion.

Takeaway:

You are being called to confront the shadows of your conscience and acknowledge how guilt may influence your thoughts, feelings, and behaviors. You are being encouraged to take responsibility for your actions, seek forgiveness and redemption, and ultimately release yourself from guilt. You can transform guilt into a catalyst for growth, healing, and personal liberation through self-reflection, accountability, and compassion.

Exercise:

Stuck with your Inner Critic

Your Inner Critic is part of your internal programming, and it's too much a part of your life to be silenced or eliminated. Oftentimes, it's this inner critic that gets you stuck in feelings of guilt.

It's created by all the internal and external criticisms you've experienced
for a lifetime, and you've strengthened it by resisting it for all these years.
So, don't waste your time thinking you will get rid of the Inner Critic. It has a lifetime membership.

Instead of fighting your Inner Critic, just accept your Inner Critic, breathe, and return to your true, authentic self. From this perspective of friendliness, care, and compassion, you'll understand that your Inner Critic is trying in a negative way to help you.

Focus on what's right about you and empathize with your humanness.

Get Unstuck from Your Inner Critic Steps

1. Sit with and accept your Inner Critic.
2. Breathe.
3. Visualize yourself returning to your true, authentic self.
4. Notice your Inner Critic from that perspective.
5. See your Inner Critic with friendliness, care, and compassion.

HABITS

Habits are the invisible threads that weave the fabric of our daily lives, shaping our thoughts, behaviors, and, ultimately, our destiny. This card delves into the patterns and routines that govern our existence, inviting us to examine the habits that serve us well and those that may be holding us back. It reminds us that we can transform our lives and create our desired future by cultivating positive habits and releasing those that no longer serve us.

Key Meanings:

Patterned Behavior: Habits are formed through repetition and reinforcement, often operating on autopilot without conscious awareness. This card encourages us to become more mindful of our habitual patterns and routines, recognizing their impact on our thoughts, emotions, and actions. By bringing awareness to our habits, we gain greater insight into ourselves and the choices we make each day.

Positive Reinforcement: When aligned with our goals and values, habits can be powerful tools for personal growth and self-improvement. This card reminds us to cultivate positive habits that support our well-being, such as regular exercise, healthy eating, mindfulness practices,
or creative pursuits. By consistently engaging in these behaviors, we strengthen our resilience, enhance productivity, and nurture a sense of fulfillment and purpose.

Breaking Unhealthy Patterns: Habits can also perpetuate negative patterns and cycles that undermine our happiness and success. This card encourages us to identify and release habits that no longer serve our highest good, whether harmful behaviors, limiting beliefs, or self-sabotaging tendencies. By breaking free from these unhealthy patterns, we create space for new possibilities to emerge and transform our lives.

Cultivating Discipline and Consistency: Habits are built upon discipline and consistency, requiring commitment and effort to maintain over time. This card reminds us of the importance of setting clear intentions, establishing routines, and staying accountable to ourselves as we work towards our goals.

By cultivating discipline and consistency in our habits, we empower ourselves to create lasting change and achieve our fullest potential.

Takeaway:

This card invites you to reflect on the patterns and routines that shape your life. It encourages you to cultivate positive habits that support your growth and well-being while releasing those that no longer serve you. By bringing awareness to your habits and making conscious choices daily, you can harness the power of repetition to create positive change and lead a more fulfilling and purposeful life.

Exercise:

Passive Relaxation

Studies have shown that 60-80% of doctor visits are stress-related. Clearly, this indicates that your wellness depends on how well you can relax through the inevitable moments of stress and tension that present themselves every day. Healthy, stress-relieving habits will help!

To relax and feel more open, you can always take a deep, satisfying let-go breath or two. Focus on the exhales; you always let go and relax when you pay a little more attention to your exhales.

To deepen your relaxation, close your eyes and focus your attention on your feet. Think about the walking you've done today and about how your feet can now rest. Imagine the tension and pressure draining from your feet. Next, visualize the flow of tension running down your calves towards your feet. Feel the stress draining out of you like warm syrup out of a bottle. Imagine your legs as large rags, wet and heavy and limp. Feel the heaviness settling from your chest into your stomach; let the sinking feeling spread throughout your abdomen.

Then, roll your head from side to side and feel the tension breaking loose from your neck and shoulders and flowing down and out. Allow any pressure to gather and flow down your arms. Let it drain from your head and face, like melting wax, flowing down your arms and hands and out your fingertips. Take a deep breath and, as you exhale, feel your arms and hands heavy with the flow of tension.

Feel the tension melting and draining out of you like warm butter.

By making this practice a habit, you can stop the dangerous and damaging habit of storing tension and stress in your body.

Passive Relaxation in 5 Easy Steps

1. Close your eyes and focus your attention on your feet and the pressure draining from them.
2. Visualize the flow of tension running down from your chest, stomach, legs, and calves.
3. Roll your head from side to side and release tension from your head, neck, and shoulders.
4. Allow tension to roll from your head and face through your arms and out your fingertips.
5. Take deep breaths, and as you exhale, feel the flow of tension escape from your hands and feet.

IMAGINATION

Imagination is the fertile ground where dreams take root and realities are woven. This card embodies the boundless realm of creativity and the infinite possibilities that arise from it. In a world governed by imagination, there are no limits, only the expansive horizon of the mind.

Key Meanings

Creativity Unleashed: Imagination is the wellspring from which creativity flows. This card encourages you to tap into your creative potential and explore new ways of expressing yourself. Whether through art, writing, music, or any other form of self-expression, allow your imagination to soar and paint your world with the colors of your dreams.

Infinite Possibilities: When you embrace the power of imagination, you open yourself up to a world of limitless possibilities. This card reminds you that there are no boundaries or constraints in the realm of the imagination. Dare to dream big and envision the life you desire, for in your mind, anything is possible.

Visualization and Manifestation: Imagination is a potent tool for manifestation.
By vividly envisioning your goals and desires, you can align your thoughts with your intentions and attract positive outcomes into your life. Use this card as a reminder to visualize your dreams with clarity and conviction, trusting in the creative energy of the universe to bring them to fruition.

Childlike Wonder: Imagination is often associated with the innocence and wonder of childhood. This card encourages you to reconnect with your inner child and embrace a sense of playfulness and curiosity. Approach life with a fresh perspective, free from preconceived notions or limitations, and allow yourself to be enchanted by the magic surrounding you.

Takeaway:

You are invited to embrace the full spectrum of your creative potential.
It encourages you to trust in your imagination's power and allow your dreams to take flight. Whether you are seeking inspiration, manifesting your desires, or simply longing to infuse your life with a sense of wonder, remember that the key lies within you. Open your mind, unleash your imagination, and watch the world transform.

Exercise:

Big Red Hot Air Balloon

This exercise requires a little imagination. Right now (and as often as you'd like), picture yourself walking in a beautiful grassy field. The sun is warm, a cool breeze is blowing, and birds float in the bright blue sky. You notice that sitting in the field is a giant red hot-air balloon you can ride in. Curious, you walk over. As you get near it, you have a fantastic idea: To put all your worry, guilt, anger, fear–all your hidden feelings–into the big wicker basket under the balloon. You fill it up, and as you do, you feel lighter.

Then, you cut the ropes holding the hot-air balloon to the ground.

As you cut the ropes, one by one, you sever the ties to all that stress.
You feel even freer, less connected to it all. And as the balloon lifts off
the ground, you still feel happier–it feels so good to see all that pressure and worry floating away!

The higher it soars, the happier and freer you feel. There goes your stress and tension as the balloon keeps drifting higher past the clouds.
Pretty soon, it's just a tiny red dot in the sky. And then it's gone. Vanished.

Say goodbye to your stressful issues, thoughts, and feelings–everything you've been carrying around inside.

The Big Red Hot-Air Balloon in 5 Easy Steps

1. Picture yourself walking in a big, grassy field on a beautiful day.
2. Notice the big red hot-air balloon.
3. Put all your hidden feelings in the basket, noticing how you feel as you load them.
4. Cut the ropes holding down the hot-air balloon filled with your stress.
5. Feel the freedom and happiness as your stress floats away into the sky.

INDEPENDENCE

The Independence card symbolizes the freedom and autonomy that comes from being self-reliant and self-sufficient. It embodies the strength and confidence to chart your own path, make your own decisions, and live according to your own values and beliefs. This card invites you to embrace your independence, stand tall in your sovereignty, and boldly pursue your dreams and aspirations.

Key Meanings:

Self-Reliance and Autonomy: Independence invites you to rely on yourself for guidance, support, and validation rather than seeking it from external sources. This card reminds you that you have the power within you to make your own choices, follow your own path, and create the life you desire. By embracing your autonomy, you free yourself from the limitations of dependence and unlock your potential for growth and self-discovery.

Courage and Confidence: Independence is rooted in courage and confidence–the courage to trust in yourself and your abilities and the confidence to pursue your goals with determination and resilience. This card encourages you to believe in yourself, knowing that you have the strength and resilience to overcome any obstacles that may arise along the way. By cultivating courage and confidence, you empower yourself to step boldly into the unknown and create the life you envision for yourself.

Freedom and Liberation: Independence represents the freedom and liberation that comes from breaking free from external constraints and living on your terms. This card reminds you that true freedom is found within by

living authentically and expressing yourself fully. By embracing your independence, you liberate yourself from the expectations and judgments of others and step into a life of authenticity, purpose,
and fulfillment.

Empowerment and Self-Expression: Ultimately, independence is about empowerment and self-expression–the ability to live in alignment with your true self and express your unique gifts and talents to the world.
This card invites you to celebrate your individuality, honor your inner wisdom, and express yourself authentically in all areas of your life.
By embracing your independence and owning your truth, you inspire others to do the same and create a ripple effect of empowerment
and liberation.

Takeaway:

Embrace your independence and stand tall in your sovereignty. Trust yourself, follow your own path, and live according to your own values and beliefs. Embrace the freedom and empowerment that comes from being independent, and watch as you step into your true power and create a life of authenticity, purpose, and fulfillment.

Exercise:

Say Your Name

Start by taking three deep belly breaths. Inhale through your nose, filling your belly first, then your chest. Then exhale, releasing your chest first, then your belly.

Continue breathing.

Next, on the exhales, say your name aloud. This may feel strange, as you may not often say your name, especially alone!

After a few rounds of this, say,

"I love you," or "I trust you," or whatever you'd like on the inhale, then say your name on the exhale.

Recognize any discomfort or awkwardness this may bring up, accept it,
and continue. If you'd like, try it while looking at yourself in the mirror!

This exercise will help you develop the self-confidence and courage to step into empowered independence.

INDIVIDUALITY

The Individuality card celebrates your unique essence and authenticity. It symbolizes the beauty and power of embracing your individuality, honoring your unique gifts, talents, and perspectives, and expressing yourself authentically. This card invites you to celebrate your uniqueness, embrace your quirks and idiosyncrasies, and shine brightly as the one-of-a-kind being that you are.

Key Meanings:

Celebration of Uniqueness: Individuality invites you to celebrate the unique qualities and attributes that make you who you are. This card reminds you that there is beauty and power in embracing your individuality and recognizing and honoring the things that set you apart. By celebrating your uniqueness, you enrich the tapestry of life with your own special flavor and contribute to the diversity and richness of the world.

Authentic Self-Expression: Individuality is about expressing yourself authentically without fear of judgment or rejection. This card encourages you to embrace your true self and express yourself boldly and unapologetically. Whether through your words, actions, or creative endeavors, allow your authentic self to shine.

Embracing Diversity: Individuality celebrates the diversity of humanity, honoring the myriad ways we each express ourselves and navigate the world. This card reminds you that diversity is a strength, not a weakness, and that we are all connected by our shared humanity while celebrating our individual differences. By embracing diversity and honoring the uniqueness of others, you create a more inclusive and compassionate world for all.

Self-Acceptance and Self-Love: Ultimately, individuality is about self-acceptance and self-love–the ability to embrace all aspects of yourself, including your flaws and imperfections, with kindness and compassion. This card invites you to love yourself unconditionally, knowing that you are worthy and deserving of love exactly as you are. By embracing your individuality and owning your truth, you empower yourself to live a life of authenticity, purpose, and fulfillment.

Takeaway:

Embrace and celebrate your uniqueness by expressing yourself authentically, honoring your individuality, and shining brightly as the one-of-a-kind being you are. Embrace the diversity and richness of your identity, and watch as you inspire others to do the same, creating a world that celebrates the beauty of individuality in all its forms.

Exercise:

Celebrate your unique qualities: take a few minutes each day to acknowledge and appreciate what sets you apart. Write down one distinctive trait or talent and how it positively impacts your life, reinforcing your sense of individuality and self-worth.

INNER BEAUTY

Inner Beauty radiates from the depths of our being, a radiant light that shines forth from the essence of who we are. This card embodies the essence of inner beauty, reminding us that true beauty lies not in our outward appearance but in the qualities of kindness, compassion, authenticity, and love that emanate from within. It invites us to honor and celebrate the unique beauty of our souls, recognizing that this inner radiance illuminates the world around us.

Key Meanings:

Authenticity and Self-Acceptance: Inner Beauty invites us to embrace our authenticity and self-acceptance, recognizing and honoring the unique qualities and gifts that make us who we are. This card reminds us that beauty comes from being true to ourselves, embracing our flaws and imperfections, and loving ourselves unconditionally.
By embracing our authenticity, we radiate a magnetic inner beauty that draws others towards us and inspires them to do the same.

Kindness and Compassion: Inner Beauty is expressed through acts of kindness and compassion, the willingness to extend love and empathy to ourselves and others. This card encourages us to cultivate a compassionate heart, treating ourselves and others with kindness, respect, and understanding. By practicing acts of kindness and compassion, we illuminate the world with the warmth and radiance of our inner beauty, creating a ripple effect of love and healing that touches all those around us.

Strength and Resilience: Inner Beauty is a source of strength and resilience, empowering us to navigate life's challenges with grace and courage. This card reminds us that true beauty is not fragile or superficial but resilient and enduring, rooted in the depths of our being. By cultivating inner strength and resilience, we tap into a wellspring of power that enables us to overcome adversity, face our fears, and emerge stronger and more radiant.

Connection to the Divine: Inner Beauty reflects our connection to the divine, the sacred essence that dwells within and around us. This card invites us to recognize the divine spark within each of us, illuminating our souls with its infinite light and love. By nurturing our connection to the divine, we align ourselves with the highest expression of inner beauty, embodying the divine qualities of love, compassion, and wisdom in all that we do.

Takeaway:

You are invited to recognize and honor the unique beauty of your soul. Embrace your authenticity, cultivate kindness and compassion, and tap into the strength and resilience that lies within you. Embrace the beauty of your soul, and watch as you illuminate the world with the radiance of your inner light.

Exercise:

Feel Your Aura

Sometimes, our receptivity allows us to pick up on the stress and negativity of others. Here's a technique that will help you stay attuned to your inner beauty, no matter who is around you.

Imagine an aura around your body. An aura is a warm, glowing light just a few inches from your body. It encloses your entire body like a soft, shining blanket that can comfort, relax, and protect you energetically. Think of it as a force field that contains positive, loving energy and keeps out unwanted negativity or stress. Only what you choose to let enter will pass through to you. You might think of this aura as made up of the radiant energy of everyone who has ever loved you, whether that be a parent, spouse, children, or even pets. You can make your aura any color you wish or even a combination of colors.

Your aura relaxes away your stress by making you feel protected and secure. Every morning, keep your eyes closed and just feel your aura. See it in your favorite color, all over your body, warming and preparing you for the day.

Throughout the day, notice your protective aura, no matter what you're doing. You can do this while driving, shopping, at home, at work, or while doing nothing–just relax into it again and again.

When you carry your aura, your imagination will unify with your body and become a tremendously positive force against stress.

Feel Your Aura in 4 Easy Steps

1. Close your eyes and imagine your aura.
2. Feel its comfort, warmth, and protective love.
3. See it in your favorite color.
4. Imagine its protection around you as you continue your day.

INSPIRATION

The Inspiration card symbolizes the spark of creativity, passion, and enthusiasm
that ignites within us, guiding us toward new ideas, insights, and possibilities. It embodies the energy of inspiration as a catalyst for growth, transformation, and manifestation. This card invites you to open yourself up to the flow of inspiration, to seek out sources of inspiration in your life, and to allow yourself to be guided by the creative muse within.

Key Meanings:

Creative Expression: Inspiration invites you to tap into your innate creativity and express yourself authentically. This card reminds you that you are a vessel for creative energy, capable of channeling inspiration into many forms through art, writing, music, dance, or any other creative endeavor. By allowing yourself to be guided
by the creative muse within, you unlock the power to inspire others and live a fulfilled life.

Clarity and Insight: Inspiration often brings clarity and insight, illuminating the path forward and revealing new possibilities. This card encourages you to pay attention
to the whispers of inspiration within you, for they may be the key to unlocking your
true potential and purpose. By following your inspiration with courage and curiosity, you open yourself to a world of infinite possibilities and opportunities for growth and expansion.

Passion and Enthusiasm: Inspiration is fueled by passion and enthusiasm—the fire that burns within us and drives us towards our goals and dreams. This card reminds you to follow your passions with zeal and enthusiasm, knowing that you are unstoppable when you are aligned with what truly lights you up. By cultivating a sense of excitement and joy in your pursuits, you infuse your life with vitality and purpose and inspire others to do the same.

Connection and Collaboration: Inspiration often flourishes in the company of others through collaboration, shared ideas, and mutual support. This card invites you to seek out sources of inspiration in your community, whether through creative workshops, brainstorming sessions, or simply connecting with like-minded individuals who share your passions and interests. By fostering connections and collaborations, you amplify the power of inspiration and create a ripple effect of creativity and innovation worldwide.

Takeaway:

Open yourself up to the flow of inspiration in your life. Embrace your creativity, follow your passions, and allow inspiration to take hold.
Embrace the magic of inspiration, and watch as you awaken to new insights, ideas, and possibilities, igniting the spark of creativity within you and realizing your deepest desires with joy and enthusiasm.

Exercise:

Look at the Sky

Whenever you need inspiration, go outside for a minute or two, take a couple of deep, let-go breaths, and look up into the sky. Without looking directly into the sun, look at the clouds, stars, or moon.

Look beyond the clouds or at the vast spaces between the stars. You'll see that the sky goes on and on, endlessly, into infinity. You can't look at the sky; you have to look *into* it. You simply look into
the sky and its depths and see it goes on forever. Possibilities are endless just like the sky.

When you focus on the vastness of the sky and see the eternal, never-ending freedom of the universe, you can feel at peace and inspired to explore what it has to offer.

Look at the Sky in 4 Easy Steps

1. Go outside and take a few deep, let-go breaths.
2. Look up at the sky without looking directly at the sun.
3. Notice the vastness of the sky.
4. Recognize the never-ending expanse of possibility in your universe.

INTEGRATION

Integration is the harmonious merging of disparate parts into a unified whole. This card represents the process of synthesis and reconciliation, where opposing forces come together to create a greater sense of balance and wholeness.
In self-discovery and growth, integration is vital in aligning our inner and outer worlds.

Key Meanings:

Wholeness and Balance: Integration invites us to acknowledge and embrace all aspects of ourselves, light and shadow. By integrating our strengths and weaknesses, joys and sorrows, we can cultivate a greater sense of wholeness and balance within. This card reminds us that true fulfillment comes from accepting ourselves in our entirety and finding harmony within the complexity of our being.

Alignment of Mind, Body, and Spirit: Integration involves aligning our thoughts, actions, and beliefs with our deepest values and intentions. When we integrate the wisdom of our intuition with the clarity of our intellect and the vitality of our physical body, we experience a profound sense of alignment and purpose. This card encourages us to cultivate a holistic approach to life, honoring mind, body, and spirit interconnectedness.

Healing and Transformation: Integration is a process of healing and transformation where we integrate past experiences and lessons into our present awareness. By acknowledging and integrating unresolved emotions, traumas, or patterns, we can release old wounds and embrace new possibilities for growth. This card reminds us that through integration, we can heal the fragments of our past and emerge stronger, wiser, and more resilient.

Unity and Connection: Integration fosters a sense of unity and connection with others and the world around us. When we recognize the interconnectedness of all beings and honor the diversity of human experience, we cultivate empathy, compassion, and understanding.
This card encourages us to seek common ground and bridge divides, recognizing that we are all part of the same tapestry of life.

Takeaway:

You are invited to embrace the process of synthesis and reconciliation
in your life. Integrate the various aspects of yourself, your experiences,
and your relationships into a cohesive whole. You'll find greater wholeness, alignment, and connection through integration, allowing you to navigate life with clarity, authenticity, and grace.

Exercise:

Take a few moments to sit quietly and reflect on areas where you feel
a disconnect between your inner desires and your outer actions. Write down one specific aspect where this disparity is most evident, such as your career, relationships, or personal habits. Next, list three actionable steps to align your actions with your true intentions.
For example, if your career doesn't reflect your passion for creativity, consider dedicating time each day to a creative hobby or exploring career options that align with your interests. Finally, visualize yourself living in harmony, where your inner values and outer life are in sync, and commit to taking these steps over the next week.

INTEGRITY

The Integrity card symbolizes aligning your thoughts, words, and actions with your deepest values and principles. It embodies the virtues of honesty, authenticity, and moral strength, guiding you to live with integrity in all areas of your life. This card invites you to cultivate a strong moral compass, honor your commitments, and stand firmly in your truth, knowing that integrity is the foundation of true character and inner peace.

Key Meanings:

Honesty and Transparency: Integrity invites you to be honest and transparent in your dealings with yourself and others. This card reminds you that honesty is the bedrock of integrity. By speaking and acting truthfully, you build trust and respect in your relationships and create a foundation of authenticity and openness. By aligning your words with your truth, you honor your integrity and cultivate deeper connections with those around you.

Consistency and Reliability: Integrity is about consistency and reliability–keeping your promises, honoring your commitments, and following through on your word. This card encourages you to be a person of your word, someone who can be
trusted to do what they say they will do, even when it's difficult or inconvenient.
By embodying reliability and dependability, you build a reputation for integrity
that precedes you and earns you the respect and admiration of others.

Moral Courage and Conviction: Integrity requires moral courage and conviction–the willingness to stand up for your beliefs, even in the face of opposition or adversity. This card reminds you to listen to the voice of your conscience and act following your deepest values and principles, even when it's not easy. By staying true to yourself and your beliefs,
you demonstrate strength of character and inspire others to do the same.

Wholeness and Integration: Ultimately, integrity is about wholeness and integration–aligning all aspects of yourself with your highest truth and purpose. This card invites you to integrate your thoughts, emotions, and actions into a harmonious whole, living with integrity in every area of your life. You experience deep inner peace and fulfillment that transcends external circumstances by aligning with your inner truth and honoring your values.

Takeaway:

Uphold your values and principles with honesty and authenticity. Live with integrity in all areas of your life, honoring your commitments, speaking your truth, and standing firmly in your convictions.
Embrace the virtue of integrity, and watch as you cultivate deeper trust, respect, and harmony in your relationships and experience a greater sense of inner peace.

Exercise:

Practice living in alignment with your values: Today, identify one core value that is important to you and set an intention to embody it throughout the day. Reflect on situations where you upheld this value, and note any moments you felt challenged. In the evening, journal about your experiences, focusing on how maintaining your integrity influenced your interactions and decisions. Do this practice regularly. Over time, observe how this practice strengthens your commitment to living authentically.

INTIMACY

The Intimacy card symbolizes the profound connection and closeness that arise from sharing our true selves with one another. It embodies the vulnerability, trust, and authenticity required to cultivate deep and meaningful relationships. This card invites you to embrace intimacy in all its forms, nurture the bonds of love and connection in your life, and create spaces of safety and acceptance where you can be fully seen and understood.

Key Meanings:

Vulnerability and Trust: Intimacy requires vulnerability and trust–the willingness to open your heart and share your true self with another, knowing that you will be held with love and acceptance. This card invites you to cultivate trust in yourself and others, let down your guard, and allow yourself to be seen and known in all your complexity and beauty. By embracing vulnerability, you create the space for deeper, richer relationships.

Authentic Communication: Intimacy is grounded in authentic communication–honesty, openness, and vulnerability in sharing your thoughts, feelings, and desires with another. This card encourages you to communicate openly and honestly with your loved ones, expressing your needs and desires with courage. By fostering clear and heartfelt communication, you deepen your connections and cultivate trust and understanding in your relationships.

Emotional Connection: Intimacy is about emotional connection–feeling deeply seen, heard, and understood by another and reciprocating that same level of empathy and understanding in return. This card reminds you to nurture emotional intimacy in your relationships, listen deeply to your loved ones' feelings and experiences, and hold space for their vulnerabilities with compassion and empathy. By cultivating emotional connection, you create a bond of love and intimacy that transcends words and actions.

Physical Affection: Intimacy can also be expressed through physical affection–touch, hugs, kisses, and other gestures of love and tenderness. This card invites you to express your affection freely and openly with your loved ones, to embrace them with warmth and tenderness, and to allow yourself to receive their love and affection in return. By honoring the physical aspect of intimacy, you deepen your connections and create a sense of closeness and belonging in your relationships.

Takeaway:

Cultivate intimacy in your relationships by embracing vulnerability, trust, and authentic communication. Nurture emotional connection and physical affection with your loved ones, creating spaces of safety and acceptance. Embrace the gift of intimacy, and watch your relationships flourish with love, trust, and understanding.

Exercise:

Vulnerable Sharing

1. Find a Safe Space: Choose a quiet, comfortable place where you feel secure and at ease. This could be a cozy corner of your home, a serene outdoor spot, or any environment that allows you to relax and open up.
2. Set an Intention: Take a few deep breaths and set an intention to be fully present and authentic during this exercise. Focus on creating a space of safety and acceptance for yourself and your partner.
3. Reflect and Share:
    - Reflection: Spend a few minutes reflecting on a personal story or experience that has shaped you. It could be a moment of joy, a challenge you overcame, or a lesson you learned. Choose something that feels meaningful and authentic.
    - Sharing: If you are with a partner, take turns sharing your stories. Speak from the heart and listen with empathy and without judgment. If you do this exercise alone, write your story in a journal or speak it aloud.
4. Express Gratitude: After sharing, express gratitude for the vulnerability and trust shown. Acknowledge the courage it takes to open up and the strength it brings to your relationship.
5. Embrace Connection: Spend a few moments in silence, simply being present with the emerging feelings and connections. Allow yourself to feel the deep intimacy of being truly seen and understood.
6. Commit to Nurturing Intimacy: Commit to continuing to nurture intimacy in your relationships. Consider setting aside regular time for deep, meaningful conversations or other activities that foster connection and closeness.

By engaging in this exercise, you cultivate intimacy and embrace the profound connections that arise from sharing your true self with others.

INTUITION

The Intuition card represents the inner knowing, wisdom, and guidance that arises from the depths of your soul. It embodies the power of intuition as a trusted ally and compass on your journey of self-discovery and growth. This card invites you to listen to your intuition's whispers, trust the insights and nudges that arise from within,
and follow the guidance of your inner wisdom with courage and conviction.

Key Meanings:

Inner Knowing: Intuition invites you to trust the wisdom within you–the innate knowing that transcends logic and reason. This card reminds you that you have a vast reservoir of wisdom and insight within yourself, waiting to be tapped into and explored. By quieting the chatter of the mind and tuning into the whispers of your intuition, you can access the guidance and clarity you need to navigate life's challenges with grace and ease.

Trust and Surrender: Intuition is rooted in trust and surrender–the willingness to let go of control and surrender to the wisdom of your true self. This card encourages you to trust the nudges and insights that arise from within, even when they defy logic or rational explanation. By surrendering to the guidance of your intuition, you open yourself up to the infinite possibilities and blessings that await you on your path.

Connection to Higher Self: Intuition is a direct line of communication with your truest self. This card reminds you to cultivate a deeper connection to your truest self through meditation, journaling, or spending time in nature. By quieting the mind and tuning in, you can receive the guidance and clarity you need to navigate life's twists and turns gracefully and easily.

Discernment and Action: Intuition invites you to discern between the whispers of your intuition and the noise of the ego and to take inspired action based on the guidance you receive. This card reminds you to trust your intuition to guide you toward your highest good, even when the path ahead may seem uncertain or challenging. By taking aligned action based on the wisdom of your intuition, you step into your power and create the life you desire with confidence and conviction.

Takeaway:

Trust the wisdom of your intuition and follow its guidance with courage and conviction. Cultivate a deeper connection to your inner knowing, quiet the mind's chatter, and tune into the whispers of your intuition with an open heart and mind. Embrace the gift of intuition, and watch as you are guided toward truth, alignment, and fulfillment on your journey of self-discovery and growth.

Exercise:

Quiet Moments

Sometimes, the best way to tap into our intuition is to find a few moments of intentional quiet. Close your mouth with your lips just touching, your teeth slightly apart, and your tongue resting on the roof of your mouth. Sit very still like this, with your lips together, for a few moments. Soon, the quiet will begin. Your thinking and mind-chatter
will stop. All you need to do is observe.

Relaxing your mouth and jaw will quiet your mind and ease your stress, allowing your intuition to be heard. Do this a few times when you need a quiet moment, and you'll soon find it happening automatically.

Quiet Moments in 3 Easy Steps

1. Close your mouth, lips just touching, teeth apart, and tongue resting on the roof of your mouth.
2. Sit still for a few moments and observe the stillness in your mind.
3. Observe your quieted mind and listen to your intuition.

JOY

The Joy card radiates with the vibrant energy of happiness, fulfillment, and contentment. It embodies the essence of joy as a state of being transcending external circumstances. This card invites us to celebrate life's simple pleasures, cultivate gratitude for the abundance that surrounds us, and embrace the fullness
of our being with open arms.

Key Meanings:

Gratitude and Appreciation: Joy invites us to cultivate gratitude and appreciation for the blessings in our lives, no matter how small. Joy is not dependent on external circumstances but arises from within. By focusing on what we are grateful for,
we shift our perspective towards abundance and invite more joy into our lives.

Presence and Mindfulness: Joy is found in the present moment when we fully immerse ourselves in the richness and beauty of life unfolding around us. Cultivate presence and mindfulness daily by bringing our attention to the here and now and savoring each moment with open-hearted awareness. By being fully present, we open ourselves up to the joy inherent in every moment.

Connection and Celebration: Joy is amplified when shared with others when we celebrate life's blessings and milestones. Cultivate joy through shared laughter, heartfelt conversations, or acts of kindness and generosity. By nurturing our connections with others, we create a ripple effect of joy that uplifts and inspires all those around us.

Inner Fulfillment and Contentment: Ultimately, joy is found within ourselves by connecting with our true essence. Explore the inner landscape of our being and connect with the source of joy within us. By cultivating self-love, self-acceptance, and inner peace, we awaken to boundless joy and experience a sense of fulfillment and contentment.

Takeaway:

Cultivate joy in your life by embracing gratitude, presence, and connection. Celebrate life's simple pleasures, nurture connections with others, and cultivate inner fulfillment and contentment. Embrace joy and illuminate the world with your radiant light and infectious enthusiasm.

Exercise:

Smell the Flowers

First, as always, notice your breathing and accept it as it is. Now, imagine traveling to a favorite place; this can be a place you love, feel comfortable in, or know well. Maybe it's somewhere you went as a child, somewhere
you go now on your own or a place you've created in your imagination,
like a tropical island or an area in the mountains with a beautiful stream.
Just imagine any quiet, sacred place.

Practice picturing this favorite place–make it detailed –and tune into every sense to stop, smell, taste, feel, see, and hear everything, including the flowers!

Smell the Flowers in 3 Easy Steps

1. Notice your breathing and accept it as it is.
2. Imagine traveling to your favorite place.
3. Practice picturing this favorite place with all the details.

KARMA

Karma is the cosmic law of cause and effect, the invisible thread that weaves together the fabric of our lives and shapes our destiny. This card embodies the essence of karma, reminding us that every action, thought, and intention carries its own energy and consequence. It invites us to become conscious co-creators of our reality, recognizing our power to shape our lives through our choices and deeds.

Key Meanings:

Law of Cause and Effect: Karma is the law of cause and effect, the principle that every action we take has positive and negative consequences that ripple into the universe and return to us in kind. This card reminds us to be mindful of our thoughts, words, and deeds, recognizing their impact on ourselves and others. By acting with intention and integrity, we align ourselves with positive karma, inviting blessings and abundance into our lives.

Responsibility and Accountability: Karma calls us to take responsibility for our actions and choices, acknowledging that we are the architects of our destiny. This card encourages us to own our mistakes and shortcomings, learn from them, and make amends where necessary. By taking responsibility for our actions and holding ourselves accountable, we empower ourselves to break free from negative patterns and create a more positive and fulfilling future.

Compassion and Forgiveness: Karma also reminds us of the importance of compassion and forgiveness in breaking the cycle of karmic patterns and healing past wounds. This card invites us to cultivate compassion for ourselves and others, recognizing that we are all on a journey of growth
and evolution. By extending forgiveness to ourselves and others, we release the hold of negative karma and create space for healing, reconciliation, and renewal.

Alignment with Higher Purpose: Karma is ultimately about aligning ourselves with our higher purpose and soul's journey, recognizing that every experience–whether positive or negative–furthers our spiritual evolution. This card encourages us to trust in the universe's wisdom
and surrender to the flow of life, knowing that everything happens for
a reason and that we are always exactly where we are meant to be. We invite positive karma's blessings and fulfill our highest potential by aligning ourselves with our soul's purpose.

Takeaway:

Be mindful of the energy you put into the world and the consequences of your actions. Take responsibility for your choices and deeds, recognizing that you can shape your lives through your thoughts, words, and actions. Embrace the wisdom of karma, and watch as you align yourself with the flow of positive energy and create a life filled with blessings, abundance, and fulfillment.

Exercise:

Reflect on karma: each evening, review your actions and interactions throughout the day, considering how they might contribute to the energy you send into the world. Write down instances where you acted with kindness and integrity and moments where you could improve.
Use these reflections to set positive intentions for the next day, fostering a cycle of good karma.

LAST ROW

The Last Row card symbolizes your truest, highest self, seated in the last row of the movie theater showing the movie of your life. It brings light to the side of ourselves that is friendly, caring, and compassionate while witnessing our life and invites us to strive toward this perspective of the Last Row–where our truest self is seated and can watch our inner critic and life movie simultaneously with love.

Key Meanings:

Friendliness: Your Last Row self watches the movie of your life and witnesses your inner critic seated in the fifteenth row. No matter what is playing on the screen or what your inner critic is saying, your last-row self is friendly and truly listening and seeing your best intentions.

Care: Your Last Row self loves and cares about you regardless of what you've done or what has happened. Your Last Row self sees you for who you truly are and deeply cares about your health, well-being, and happiness.

Compassion: No matter what's happening in the movie of your life, your Last Row self has compassion toward you and loves you unconditionally. They recognize the difficulty and suffering in your life and want what's best for you.

Empathy: Your Last Row self fully understands and feels your experience and perspective. When you sit in the Last Row of your Inner Theater, you can look upon the movie of your life with empathy and grace, loving yourself unconditionally despite challenges, mistakes, and setbacks. You can also look upon your inner critic in the fifteenth row and empathize with how they feel and why they feel their criticism is self-preserving or egoic.

The Inner Critic: The inner critic is the other one in the theater. When you are practicing the exercise of entering your Inner Theater, you may find yourself seated with your inner critic before you can move up to the Last Row. This is fine. Take your time with your inner critic, but always be sure you end up in the Last Row.

Takeaway:

Your truest, highest self, is seated in the last row of the movie theater showing the movie of your life. This is the side of yourself that is friendly, caring, and compassionate while witnessing your life from the Last Row of your movie theater. The Last Row self can watch your inner critic in the fifteenth row and your life movie simultaneously with friendliness, care,
and compassion. Always end in the Last Row, where you view yourself and your life with unconditional love.

Exercise:

Move to the Last Row

Practice visualizing a Movie Theater that is playing the movie of your life. In that theater, you will find your inner critic in the fifteenth row and your highest self in the last row. Witness what is playing on the screen, whether it's something from the past or in the present.

What is your inner critic saying? What is your Last Row self saying?

Take the time to witness and acknowledge what each part of yourself says and thinks, then move from the Fifteenth Row to the Last Row.
You may find yourself making the walk from the fifteenth row to the last row often. This is fine and expected!

No matter what, always end in the Last Row. It's natural to spend time with your fifteenth-row inner critic, but striving toward the Last Row perspective and ending there will enable you to live a life of self-love, compassion, care, and less stress.

LAUGHTER

Laughter is the soul's music, a joyful expression of lightness and mirth that uplifts the spirit and nourishes the heart. This card embodies the essence of laughter, reminding us of the power of humor, playfulness, and lightheartedness to bring joy and vitality into our lives. It invites us to embrace laughter as a healing balm for the soul, allowing us to let go of seriousness and embrace the beauty of laughter in all its forms.

Key Meanings:

Joy and Playfulness: Laughter celebrates joy and playfulness, inviting us to embrace the childlike wonder and spontaneity within us. This card encourages us to infuse our lives with moments of lightheartedness and fun, finding joy in simple pleasures and playful interactions with others. By embracing the spirit of playfulness, we cultivate a sense of joy and vitality that uplifts our spirits and nourishes our souls.

Stress Relief and Relaxation: Laughter is also a powerful tool for stress relief and relaxation, offering a natural antidote to the pressures and worries of everyday life. This card reminds us of the healing power of laughter to lighten our burdens, dissolve tension, and promote a sense of well-being. Embracing laughter daily creates space for relaxation, rejuvenation, and inner peace.

Connection and Bonding: Laughter is a universal language bridging divides and fostering connection and bonding with others. This card encourages us to share laughter and joy with friends, family, and loved ones, deepening our connections and strengthening our relationships. By laughing together, we create bonds of love and camaraderie that uplift and sustain us through life's challenges.

Perspective and Resilience: Laughter offers a fresh perspective and a resilient spirit in the face of adversity, helping us to find lightness and humor even in difficult times. This card invites us to embrace laughter as a tool for resilience, allowing us to see the lighter side of life's challenges and setbacks. By cultivating a sense of humor and perspective, we tap into an inner reservoir of strength and resilience that helps us navigate life's ups and downs with grace and optimism.

Takeaway:

Embrace the gift of laughter, allowing yourself to find joy, humor, and lightness in life's journey. Cultivate moments of playfulness, connection, and merriment, knowing that laughter is a source of joy and a powerful medicine for the soul. Embrace the spirit of laughter, and watch as your world becomes infused with greater joy, vitality, and love.

Exercise:

Speak Gibberish

Here's a way to boost your positive self-talk and get a good laugh!

Try speaking in the universal and ridiculous language called Gibberish.

You've spoken it before: When you were a baby! You communicated an effortless flow of Gibberish, and it calmed you, delighted you, made you giggle, and quieted your mind.

So, try it! Do it aloud. If that was fun, do it again. If it felt awkward or uncomfortable, that's okay. Do it alone, so there's no one to worry about. Your Gibberish will be spontaneous and different every time you do it. However it comes out is perfect.

Some people find it hard at first to feel playful enough to speak Gibberish because they will critique and judge themselves. But hang
in there. Try speaking Gibberish aloud (even if you just mumble it) for a minute, and especially whenever you feel stressed or caught up
in negative thoughts and feelings.

This exercise will help you laugh. When was the last time you've felt this relaxed, childlike, playful, and funny?

Speak Gibberish in 4 Easy Steps

1. Speak Gibberish aloud, even if you just mumble it.
2. How long can you go? Can you sing in Gibberish?
3. Note how you feel.

LET GO

Letting go is a powerful journey of surrender and release, inviting us to relinquish what no longer serves us and make space for new beginnings to unfold. This card embodies the essence of letting go, reminding us of the liberating power of releasing attachments, expectations, and fears that weigh heavy on our hearts and minds. It invites us to trust in the natural flow of life, surrender to the universe's wisdom, and allow life to unfold gracefully and with ease.

Key Meanings:

Release of Attachments: Letting go involves releasing attachments to people, situations, and outcomes that no longer serve our highest good. This card encourages us to examine the attachments that weigh heavy on our hearts and minds, whether material possessions, relationships, or beliefs, and release them with love and compassion.

By relinquishing attachments, we create space for greater freedom, joy, and fulfillment to enter our lives.

Surrender to the Present Moment: Letting go is also about surrendering to the present moment, releasing the need to control or manipulate outcomes, and trusting in the natural flow of life. This card reminds us of the power of surrender, inviting us to let go of worries about the past or anxieties about the future and to embrace the beauty and richness of the present moment. By surrendering to the flow of life, we find peace, clarity, and serenity in the here and now.

Emotional Release and Healing: Letting go is a process of emotional release and healing, allowing us to acknowledge and express our feelings honestly and with compassion.

This card encourages us to release pent-up emotions, whether grief, anger, or fear and allows us to feel and process them fully. By honoring our emotions and letting them flow freely, we create space for healing and transformation.

Trust in Divine Timing: Letting go involves trusting in the universe's wisdom and surrendering to divine timing. This card reminds us that everything unfolds in its own time and in its own way, according to a higher plan that we may not always understand. By letting go of the need to force outcomes or control circumstances, we open ourselves up to the infinite possibilities and blessings that await us when we trust in the flow of life.

Takeaway:

This card encourages you to release attachments, surrender to the present moment, and trust in the natural flow of life. It invites you to let go of that which no longer serves you with love and compassion, freeing yourself from the burdens of the past and the anxieties of the future. Embrace the spirit
of letting go, and watch as you find greater peace, freedom, and joy in life's journey.

Exercise:

Entrance-Exit Technique

Make yourself comfortable and focus on your inhale and exhale. This is always a great place to start.

Now, think of your inhale as an entrance and your exhale as an exit. Inhale entrance, exhale exit. Repeat the entrance and exit until you get into a nice cadence.

Next, inhale as you focus on your body. From your toes to the top of your head, squeeze and feel the tension in your whole body. Clench your toes. Squeeze your hands into fists. Close your eyes tightly. Close your mouth and clamp your jaw. Lift your shoulders.

Hold the tension as long as you can, then exhale. *Exit* from the pressure, let go and relax. Allow everything to open and become loose.

Then, do it again. Bring in the tension with your breath. *Enter* into it. Squeeze everything, your hands, eyes, feet, legs, buttocks, and belly, and hold it. Lift your shoulders toward the top of your head. When you're ready, when you can't hold it any longer, exhale and *exit*. Entrance-Exit.

Repeat this as often as you'd like, holding it a bit longer each time.

In this exercise, you don't ignore, avoid, or deny your stress. You do just the opposite! You inhale and enter into your tension, you even exaggerate your tension, and then you exhale and let it go. In and out. Entrance and exit. Stress and relaxation. Holding on, then letting go.

Entrance-Exit in 5 Easy Steps

1. Think of your inhale as an entrance and your exhale as an exit. Breathe.
2. Inhale, focus on your body, and tense up your body as much as possible. Hold.
3. Exhale, exit, and release all your tension. Relax.
4. Repeat steps 2 and 3, holding a bit longer each time.
5. Notice your body and the release of tension.

LOVE

Love is the universal language of the heart, a boundless force that unites us in connection, compassion, and understanding. This card embodies the essence of love, reminding us of the transformative power of love to heal, uplift, and inspire. It invites us to open our hearts to the love that surrounds us–in all its forms–and to cultivate love as the guiding principle in our thoughts, words, and actions.

Key Meanings:

Unconditional Acceptance: Love is the gift of unconditional acceptance, the willingness to embrace ourselves and others exactly as we are, flaws and all. This card encourages us to cultivate self-love and acceptance, recognizing the inherent worth and dignity of every being. By embracing ourselves with compassion and kindness, we create a foundation of love from which we can extend love to others.

Compassion and Empathy: Love is expressed through acts of compassion and empathy, the ability to see and understand the experiences and feelings of others with kindness and understanding. This card invites us to cultivate empathy in our relationships, listening deeply to the stories and struggles of those around us with an open heart and mind. Practicing empathy and compassion fosters deeper connections, understanding, and unity with others.

Connection and Unity: Love is the force that binds us together in unity and connection, transcending differences of race, religion, or background. This card reminds us of our interconnectedness with all living beings and the earth itself, inviting us to honor and respect the web of life that sustains us. By fostering a sense of connection and unity with others, we create a more loving and compassionate world for all.

Gratitude and Generosity: Love is expressed through gratitude and generosity, the willingness to freely give ourselves and our resources to benefit others. This card encourages us to cultivate gratitude and generosity, recognizing and appreciating the abundance of love surrounding us. By sharing our love and blessings with others, we create a ripple effect of kindness and joy that uplifts and enriches the lives of all.

Takeaway:

You are invited to open your heart to the love surrounding you and cultivate love as the guiding principle in your life. Embrace love in all its forms–self-love, compassion, empathy, and generosity–and share your love freely with others. Embrace the spirit of love, and watch as your world becomes infused with greater joy, connection, and harmony.

Exercise:

Affirmation: "I open my heart to give and receive love, nurturing connections that bring joy and fulfillment into my life."

LOYALTY

Loyalty is the steadfast bond that binds hearts together, a sacred commitment to stand by one another through thick and thin. This card embodies the essence of loyalty, reminding us of the power of unwavering support, trust, and devotion in our relationships. It invites us to cultivate loyalty in our connections with others, honoring the bonds of friendship, love, and kinship that enrich our lives.

Key Meanings:

Trust and Reliability: Loyalty is built on trust and reliability, a mutual commitment to honor our word and stand by those we care about. This card encourages us to cultivate trustworthiness in our relationships, demonstrating consistency, integrity, and dependability in our words and actions. By earning the trust of others and staying true to our commitments, we strengthen the bonds of loyalty that unite us.

Support and Encouragement: Loyalty is expressed through support, encouragement, and solidarity with those we care about. This card reminds us of the importance of being there for others in need, offering a listening ear, a shoulder to lean on, or a helping hand when needed most. By showing up for others with kindness and compassion, we affirm the depth of our loyalty and strengthen the bonds of connection that unite us.

Faithfulness and Devotion: Loyalty involves a deep sense of faithfulness and devotion to those we hold dear, a commitment to prioritize their well-being and happiness above our own. This card invites us to cultivate a spirit of devotion in our relationships, nurturing the bonds of love, friendship, and kinship that sustain us. By honoring our commitments and remaining steadfast in our affections, we deepen the bonds of loyalty and create a foundation of trust and security in our relationships.

Mutual Respect and Understanding: Loyalty is rooted in mutual respect and understanding, a willingness to see and appreciate the unique qualities and perspectives of those we care about. This card encourages us to cultivate empathy, compassion, and acceptance in our relationships, honoring the differences that make each individual special. By embracing diversity and celebrating each person's strengths, we foster a culture of inclusivity and belonging that strengthens the bonds of loyalty and unity.

Takeaway:

This card reminds you to honor the bonds of trust, support, and devotion that unite you with those you hold dear. Cultivate loyalty in your relationships, demonstrating steadfastness, reliability, and commitment in your words and actions. Embrace the spirit of loyalty, and watch as your connections deepen, your bonds strengthen, and your heart expands with love and gratitude.

Exercise:

Reflect on your closest relationships and inventory your loyalty to each person. Are you trustworthy, reliable, supportive, and encouraging?
Is there mutual respect and understanding, as well as faithfulness and devotion? Are any of these components of loyalty lacking, and if so,
how could you get back on track?

MEDITATION

Meditation is a journey inward, a practice of stillness and presence that opens the gateway to inner peace, clarity, and self-discovery. This card embodies the essence of meditation, inviting us to quiet the mind, calm the spirit, and connect with the deepest aspects of our being. It reminds us that within the sanctuary of silence, we can find refuge from the chaos of the external world and tap into the boundless wellspring of wisdom and insight that resides within.

Key Meanings:

Stillness and Presence: Meditation is a practice of being fully present in the moment, cultivating a sense of inner stillness and presence that transcends the mind's noise. This card encourages us to quiet the chatter of our thoughts and turn inward, tuning into the subtle rhythms of our breath and the sensations of our bodies. We create space for clarity, insight, and inner peace by cultivating stillness and presence.

Inner Exploration and Self-Discovery: Meditation is a journey of self-exploration and discovery, offering a mirror through which we can glimpse the depths of our being. This card invites us to explore the landscape of our inner world with curiosity and compassion, observing our thoughts and emotions without judgment. By embracing the practice of meditation, we gain insight into ourselves and the patterns that shape our lives, fostering greater self-awareness and understanding.

Stress Reduction and Relaxation: Meditation is a powerful tool for stress reduction and relaxation, offering a sanctuary of peace and calm during life's challenges. This card reminds us of meditation's healing power to soothe the nervous system, quiet the mind, and promote a sense of inner tranquility. Incorporating meditation into our daily lives can reduce stress, anxiety, and tension, fostering greater resilience and well-being.

Connection to Spirituality: Meditation is also a gateway to spirituality, offering a direct experience of the divine presence that dwells within and around us. This card encourages us to cultivate a spiritual practice of meditation, connecting with the sacred essence of life and tapping into the universe's wisdom. By quieting the mind and opening the heart, we can deepen our connection to the divine and experience a profound sense of unity and wholeness.

Takeaway:

Embrace meditation as a pathway to inner peace, clarity, and self-discovery. Carve out sacred time for stillness and reflection, nurturing your connection to the deepest aspects of yourself and the universe. Embrace the practice of meditation, and watch as your life becomes infused with greater serenity, wisdom, and spiritual insight.

Exercise:

Turning Points

For the next few breaths while you read, focus on your breathing, on the rhythm of your breathing, and the rise and fall of each breath. Remember: *how* you're breathing is not important. Deep or shallow, nose or mouth, rough or smooth–it really doesn't matter. Simply notice your breathing – inhale, exhale; inhale, exhale – and accept it as it is.

After a few breaths, to take this even deeper, notice the brief pause between exhale and inhale. These are your turning points, and they're in every breath you'll ever take and have ever taken. They last about a millisecond unless you hold your breath.

For this exercise, just observe these turning points without trying to change them. Notice when they come, how long they last, and when they begin to turn. Inhale-*turn*, exhale-*turn*; inhale-*turn*, exhale-*turn*. If you're very quiet and very attentive, you might even notice that there's the tiniest space in the middle of each turning point, a split-second moment of silence poised between the inhale and the exhale.

Observing your turning points reveals something extraordinary, something very grand and straightforward at the same time. Your mind calms, your body relaxes, your hurry and busyness slow down, and you feel peace with yourself.

Turning Points in 4 Easy Steps

1. Follow steps 1 - 5 of Letting Go.
2. Notice your Turning Points when the inhale turns into an exhale and vice versa.
3. Observe your Turning Points and the quiet space between them.
4. Feel your shift towards calmness and self-acceptance.

MIND

The mind is a vast landscape of thoughts, beliefs, and perceptions that shape our reality and influence our experiences. This card delves into the depths of the mind, inviting us to explore the power of our thoughts and their role in creating our lives. It reminds us that by cultivating mindfulness and harnessing the power of our thoughts, we can transform our reality and unlock the limitless potential of our minds.

Key Meanings:

Awareness and Presence: The mind is a powerful tool for perception and understanding but can also be a source of distraction and illusion. This card encourages us to cultivate mindfulness and awareness, becoming conscious of the thoughts and beliefs that shape our reality. By bringing awareness to our mental processes, we gain greater clarity and insight into ourselves and the world around us.

Positive Thinking and Affirmation: The mind has the power to shape our reality through the thoughts and beliefs we hold. This card reminds us of the importance of cultivating positive thinking and affirming beliefs that support our well-being and success. By harnessing the power of positive thinking, we can reprogram our minds for success, abundance, and happiness, manifesting our desires with clarity and intention.

Mind-Body Connection: The mind and body are intricately connected, with thoughts and emotions influencing physical health and well-being. This card encourages us to pay attention to this connection and recognize the impact of our thoughts and beliefs on our health and vitality. By cultivating a positive mindset and releasing negative thought patterns, we can promote healing, vitality, and well-being in mind and body.

Creative Visualization and Manifestation: The mind is a powerful tool for creation and manifestation, allowing us to visualize and manifest our desires into reality. This card invites us to harness the power of creative visualization, imagining our dreams and goals with clarity and intention. By aligning our thoughts, beliefs, and actions with our desires, we can manifest our dreams into reality and create a life of purpose, passion, and fulfillment.

Takeaway:

Remember the power of your thoughts and beliefs to shape your reality. Cultivate mindfulness, positive thinking, and creative visualization, harnessing the power of your mind to manifest your desires and create the life you envision. Embrace the power of your mind, and watch as your thoughts transform into reality, unlocking the limitless potential within you.

Exercise:

Big Red Hot Air Balloon

Right now (and as often as you'd like), picture yourself walking in a beautiful grassy field. The sun is warm, a cool breeze is blowing, and birds float in the bright blue sky. You notice that sitting in the field is a giant red hot-air balloon you can ride in. Curious, you walk over. As you get near it, you have a fantastic idea: To put all your worry, guilt, anger, fear–all your hidden feelings–into the big wicker basket under the balloon. You fill it up, and as you do, you feel lighter.

Then, you cut the ropes holding the hot-air balloon to the ground. As you cut the ropes, one by one, you sever the ties to all that stress. You feel even freer, less connected to it all. And as the balloon lifts off the ground, you still feel happier–it feels so good to see all that pressure and worry floating away!

The higher it soars, the happier and freer you feel. There goes your stress and tension as the balloon keeps drifting higher past the clouds. Pretty soon, it's just a tiny red dot in the sky. And then it's gone. Vanished.

Say goodbye to your stressful issues, thoughts, and feelings–everything you've been carrying around in your mind.

The Big Red Hot-Air Balloon in 5 Easy Steps

1. Picture yourself walking in a big, grassy field on a beautiful day.
2. Notice the big red hot-air balloon.
3. Put all your hidden feelings in the basket, noticing how you feel as you load them.
4. Cut the ropes holding down the hot-air balloon filled with your stress.
5. Feel the freedom and happiness as your stress floats away into the sky.

MIND-BODY HEALING

Mind-body healing is the gentle dance of harmony between our thoughts, emotions, and physical well-being, inviting us to explore the profound connection between mind and body. This card embodies the essence of holistic healing, reminding us of the innate wisdom of our bodies and the power of our minds to promote healing and wholeness. It invites us to cultivate a deeper awareness of the mind-body connection and embrace practices that nurture our well-being on all levels.

Key Meanings:

Awareness and Integration: Mind-body healing begins with awareness of the interconnectedness between our thoughts, emotions, and physical sensations. This card encourages us to explore the subtle cues and signals that our bodies send us, recognizing the impact of our thoughts and emotions on our physical well-being. By integrating mind-body awareness, we can cultivate greater harmony and balance.

Emotional Release and Healing: The body can store and release emotional energy, impacting our health and vitality. This card reminds us of the importance of emotional release and healing, allowing us to express and process our emotions healthily. By acknowledging and releasing stored emotions, we create space for healing and transformation on both a physical and emotional level.

Mindful Practices for Healing: Mind-body healing encompasses a variety of practices and modalities that promote holistic well-being, such as meditation, yoga, tai chi, and energy healing. This card encourages us to explore these mindful practices and find those that resonate with us, nurturing our well-being on all levels. By incorporating these practices into our daily lives, we support the body's natural healing abilities and cultivate greater vitality, resilience, and peace of mind.

Self-Care and Nourishment: Mind-body healing also involves caring for our bodies and minds with love and compassion, nourishing ourselves with healthy food, rest, and relaxation. This card reminds us of the importance of self-care and self-love in promoting healing and well-being. By honoring our bodies' needs and prioritizing our well-being, we create a foundation for vibrant health and vitality to flourish.

Takeaway:

Honor the connection between your thoughts, emotions, and physical well-being. Embrace practices that nurture holistic healing, supporting the body's natural ability to heal and restore balance. Embrace the journey of mind-body healing, and watch as your life becomes infused with greater vitality, harmony, and well-being on all levels.

Exercise:

Belly Breathing

Try taking some belly breaths. First, place one hand on your chest and the other on your belly beneath your rib cage. Inhale through your nose to the count of four, letting your belly swell outward so it moves your hand. Consciously allow the belly to take in the breath, not the chest. The hand on your chest should not move. Hold your breath for a count of four. Now exhale through your mouth to a count of four.

Exhale completely–throw out all the air and allow your hand to feel your belly fall. Push your exhale by contracting your internal muscles as if blowing up a balloon, and hear the "whoosh" of air as you exhale. Allow your shoulders to drop and let go of any other tension you may be holding in your body or face. Don't worry about your exhale sounds or what your stomach looks like; this breathing is for your health!

Take four or five belly breaths and feel free to change the rhythm. As you practice, hold your breath an extra beat or make the exhales much slower. Find a comfortable rhythm for yourself. If you feel dizzy, stop for a few seconds before continuing.

Don't feel a need to breathe so deeply that your lungs burn. The whole experience should be soothing and relaxing.

Slow, full, rhythmic breathing automatically lowers your heart rate, reduces blood pressure, and relaxes your muscles. It also reduces cortisol (the stress hormone!)
in the body and calms the mind. You'll find you can give yourself some love and do belly breathing anywhere and anytime you feel tense or pressured.

Belly Breathing in 6 Easy Steps

1. Place one hand on your chest and the other on your belly.
2. Inhale through your nose to the count of four, letting your belly swell outward.
3. Hold your breath for a count of four.
4. Exhale powerfully, contracting the belly and its muscles to let out all the air.
5. Release tension with the exhale.
6. Repeat steps 2 - 5, changing the rhythm if you'd like and noticing your shift.

OPENNESS

Openness is the gateway to growth, the willingness to embrace new experiences, perspectives, and possibilities with curiosity and receptivity. This card embodies the essence of openness, inviting us to expand our minds, hearts, and spirits to the richness and diversity of life. It reminds us that cultivating openness in our lives invites the gifts of wisdom, connection, and transformation.

Key Meanings:

Curiosity and Exploration: Openness is fueled by curiosity, a desire to explore new ideas, experiences, and perspectives with an open mind and heart. This card encourages us to cultivate a spirit of curiosity, remaining open to the wonders and mysteries surrounding us. By embracing curiosity, we expand our horizons, deepen our understanding, and enrich our lives with new insights
and discoveries.

Vulnerability and Authenticity: Openness requires vulnerability–the willingness to be seen, heard, and known for who we truly are. This card reminds us to embrace authenticity and share our truth with others.

By opening ourselves up to vulnerability, we invite deeper connections, intimacy, and understanding in our relationships, fostering greater trust and authenticity.

Flexibility and Adaptability: Openness involves a willingness to adapt and respond with flexibility to life's changing circumstances. This card encourages us to embrace change with grace and resilience, trusting in the flow of life to guide us on our journey. By remaining flexible and open to new possibilities, we navigate life's twists and turns with ease and grace, embracing the opportunities for growth and transformation that arise along the way.

Empathy and Compassion: Openness fosters empathy and compassion,
the ability to see and understand the perspectives and experiences of others with empathy and kindness. This card invites us to cultivate empathy in our relationships, listening deeply to the stories and feelings of those around us with an open heart and mind. By practicing empathy and compassion, we foster deeper connections, understanding, and unity with others, creating a more compassionate and inclusive world for all.

Takeaway:

Cultivate openness in your life by embracing new experiences, perspectives, and possibilities with curiosity and receptivity. Expand your mind, heart, and spirit to the richness and diversity of life, inviting in the gifts of wisdom, connection, and transformation that
come from embracing the unknown. Embrace the spirit of openness,
and watch as your world expands with new insights, experiences, and opportunities for growth and connection.

Exercise:

Embrace the present moment with openness: spend a few minutes each day practicing mindfulness, fully experiencing your surroundings without judgment. As you do, journal about any new perspectives or feelings that arise, welcoming them with openness as opportunities for growth and connection.

PCE (POSITIVE CHILDHOOD EXPERIENCES)

The ACE Study, conducted by the Centers for Disease Control and Prevention (CDC) and Kaiser Permanente in the late 1990s, examined the correlation between adverse childhood experiences and long-term health outcomes. It highlighted the importance of addressing childhood trauma and promoting resilience as key factors in preventing and mitigating the impact of adverse experiences on health and well-being.

In contrast, PCEs (Positive Childhood Experiences) are nurturing and supportive experiences that help buffer the impact of stress and trauma, contributing to resilience and long-term well-being.

Positive experiences can build resilience, help you recover from the impacts of ACEs, and foster strong mental and physical health. Research suggests that having several PCEs can greatly reduce the likelihood of negative outcomes even in the presence of ACEs.

While ACEs can create long-lasting challenges, PCEs can serve as protective factors that promote healing, resilience, and overall well-being.

Key Meanings:

PCEs focus on nurturing and supportive experiences that help buffer the impact of stress and trauma, contributing to resilience and long-term well-being. Some common PCEs include:

1. Supportive relationships with family members and adults outside the home
2. Feeling safe and protected at home and in the community
3. Feeling heard and valued by caregivers
4. Opportunities for play and learning within a supportive environment
5. Sense of belonging within school, family, and the community
6. Developing skills to handle emotions and challenges

Takeaway:

The PCEs card highlights the positive childhood experiences that may have impacted our lives. It signifies the importance of acknowledging, understanding, and appreciating these experiences and their impact on our health and well-being. This card invites us to embark on a journey of self-discovery, healing, and resilience with the help of our past's positive learnings and lessons.

Exercise:

To determine your PCE score, take the PCE assessment, which is available
in the "Resources" section of this book.

Be sure to take a moment to reflect and answer the final questions, which are extremely helpful in beginning to resolve trauma associated
with adverse childhood experiences and stopping their negative effect
on your life.

PEACE OF MIND

The Peace of Mind card embodies the tranquility and calm that comes from inner serenity and mental clarity. It symbolizes being free from worry, stress, and inner turmoil, allowing you to experience a deep sense of peace and balance. This card invites you to cultivate practices and mindsets that foster a calm and centered state of being, embracing the serenity that comes from a quiet and harmonious mind.

Key Meanings:

Inner Calm: Finding moments of stillness and tranquility can help you manage stress and anxiety. Practices such as meditation, deep breathing, and mindfulness can support you in achieving a serene state of mind.

Mental Clarity: Peace of mind involves achieving mental clarity and focus. Clear away mental clutter and distractions to think more clearly and make better decisions. A clear mind enhances your ability to respond to challenges with composure and wisdom.

Emotional Balance: Manage your emotions in a healthy way, avoiding extremes
and finding a stable equilibrium. Emotional balance contributes to a sense of inner peace and well-being.

Harmony and Serenity: Achieving peace of mind involves creating a harmonious and serene environment, both internally and externally. Seek out and nurture spaces and relationships that promote calm and positivity. By fostering harmony, you support your overall sense of peace.

Takeaway:

Prioritize your mental and emotional well-being. Seek practices and mindsets that promote inner calm, mental clarity, and emotional balance. Consider how you can create a more serene environment and nurture relationships that support your peace of mind. By embracing tranquility and harmony, you can enhance your overall sense of
well-being and live a more balanced and fulfilling life.

Exercise:

Say Your Name

Close your eyes, focus on your breathing, and just accept your breathing as it is. After a few breaths, on an exhale, say your name to yourself,
but not out loud. Do it again. Inhale, and on the exhale, say your name
to yourself. Continue doing this for several breaths.

Once you're in a nice rhythm, on the inhales, say, "I accept" or "I care about" or "I believe in" or even "I love" and on the exhales, say your name. Do this for five to ten breaths. This is a mantra of positive
self-affirmation and peace of mind. Do it every day for a week, and notice how much more relaxed and accepting of yourself you are. With more self-love and positive self-talk, you'll enjoy more peace of mind than ever.

Say Your Name in 6 Easy Steps

1. Close your eyes, focus on your breathing and accept it as-is.
2. On an exhale, say your name in your mind.
   Repeat for several breaths.
3. On the inhales, say something loving and compassionate, starting with "I."
4. Say your name on the exhales.
5. Repeat steps 3 and 4 for 5 -10 breaths.
6. Repeat this process daily and note how you feel.

PERFECT

The Perfect card symbolizes perfection and how it impacts your life and perceptions. It reflects the pursuit of excellence, the desire for flawlessness, and the recognition that true perfection is often an illusion. This card invites you to embrace your imperfections and find beauty in growth and development, acknowledging that striving for perfection can sometimes hinder your progress and happiness.

Key Meanings:

Pursuit of Excellence: Striving to do your best and aiming for high standards is admirable, but it is important to balance this pursuit with self-compassion and realistic expectations. Excellence is about progress and effort rather than absolute flawlessness.

Acceptance of Imperfection: True perfection often includes accepting imperfections. Embrace your flaws and the imperfections of others, recognizing that they contribute to uniqueness and authenticity. By accepting imperfections, you can cultivate a healthier and more compassionate mindset.

Illusion of Perfection: Reflect on how the ideal of perfection might be influencing your thoughts and actions. Unrealistic standards can lead to unnecessary stress and dissatisfaction. Acknowledging that perfection is often an unattainable ideal allows you to focus on growth and improvement.

Beauty in Process: Perfection can be found in the process of growth and development. Appreciate the journey rather than solely focusing on the end result. By finding beauty in the process, you can enjoy each step and celebrate your progress along the way.

Takeaway:

Reflect on your relationship with perfection. Strive for excellence while embracing imperfections and recognizing the beauty in growth and development. Consider how the illusion of perfection might be impacting your life and take steps to balance high standards with self-compassion. Doing so can cultivate a more fulfilling and realistic approach to your goals and experiences.

Exercise:

Embrace the Beauty of Imperfection

The next time you feel stress building inside because of an expectation of perfection, close your eyes and focus on breathing. Don't try to change
your breathing pattern; simply accept how it is. Explore your expectations, and let go of the need for things to be perfect.

After just a few breaths, you'll be more relaxed and comfortable.

Soon, you'll come to trust that with more awareness, you can accept and embrace the beauty of imperfection.

Embracing the Beauty of Imperfection in 3 Easy Steps

1. Close your eyes and turn your attention to your breathing.
2. Accept your breathing as it is.
3. After a few minutes, note how you feel.
   Are you feeling more accepting?

PRESENT

The Present card embodies the essence of living fully in the current moment, appreciating the now, and finding joy and contentment in your immediate surroundings and experiences. It symbolizes mindfulness, awareness, and the beauty of being present. This card invites you to let go of distractions and past regrets, urging you to embrace the present moment with open-hearted attention and gratitude.

Key Meanings:

Mindfulness and Awareness: Focus on the here and now, noticing the details and beauty of your current experience. Mindfulness enhances your connection to life and fosters a more profound sense of presence.

Letting Go of Distractions: Release worries about the past and anxieties about the future, allowing yourself to fully engage with what is happening right now. By doing so, you free up mental space and energy.

Appreciation and Gratitude: Cherish your life's simple joys and blessings, cultivating a sense of gratitude for what you have. Recognizing and savoring these moments enhances your overall well-being and happiness.

Embracing Life's Richness: Be open to each moment's experiences and opportunities, finding joy and meaning in the present. You create a more vibrant and fulfilling existence by fully engaging with life.

Takeaway:

Bring your focus back to the current moment and embrace the beauty of the present. Practice mindfulness, letting go of past regrets and future anxieties. Consider how you can be more present in your daily life through mindful practices, gratitude, or simply taking time to appreciate your surroundings. Living fully in the present enhances your connection to life and experiences greater joy and contentment.

Exercise:

Going to the Movies

Start by imagining a movie theater. Visualize all the theater details – the smell of popcorn, the red velvet curtains, the dim lighting, the comfortable seats – maybe it's an IMAX theater or one with reclining seats! You enter the theater, choose your seat, get settled, and the movie has already started. But this time, the movie on the big screen is all about you.

You're the star, and it's your story. It's your work life, home life, performance, and how you deal with people, demands, success, and failure. It's a movie about your whole life.

Sitting in the 15th row – right in the middle of the theater – is your Inner Critic. This is the judgmental, controlling, never satisfied part of you. We all have this Inner Critic watching our movie, ready to tell us everything that's wrong with us.

But there's another "you" in the theater, too, sitting quietly in the last row of the theater: your Last Row Self. Your Last Row Self is your wisdom, creativity, and freedom. It's the "you" when you feel calm and peaceful, and where you can look at your movie, and at your Inner Critic in the 15th row, with understanding and love.

The Three Perspectives When You Go to the Movies

1.) You as the Star of the Movie: working, playing, driving, shopping, dealing with bosses, raising kids, keeping schedules, and feeling pushed, hurried, and stressed.
2.) Your Inner Critic in the 15th row: ready to find fault and punish you for your mistakes. The part of you that gets stuck in stress.
3.) The Last Row: the friendly, caring, and compassionate part of you that loves yourself just as you are, including your Inner Critic.

Going to the Movies in Three Steps

Now that you know the concept of "Going to the Movies" and can visualize your inner theater, it's time to practice. Whenever you feel upset, tense, or stressed out, do these three steps in order:

Step 1 - Be in your movie. Be present in the moment and experience what's happening in your movie. Let the scene unfold; feel yourself acting your role. After all, you're the star! Let yourself express your stress: "I'm in trouble.... I'm way behind, and there's no way I can catch up!"
"I'm going to be late!" "How am I going to make this month's payment?"
Let yourself think and feel everything that's going on in the scene.

Step 2 - Now, move your awareness to the 15th row. Let your Inner Critic criticize the scene. From the 15th row, focus on what's wrong with you and your thoughts and feelings: "Stop whining and get to work." "You should've started earlier." "Why did you buy it in the first place?" Let your Inner Critic be hostile and have its say.

Step 3 - Get up and walk back to the last row of the theater. Visualize yourself getting up and physically moving. There, in the last row, watch your movie and your 15th-row Inner Critic with detachment. Become aware and accept your breathing to help transport yourself to the last-row perspective–free, calm, peaceful, relaxed, observant, comfortable with yourself, friendly, caring, and compassionate.

Keep coming back to this technique. Going to the last row is coming home to YOU in the present moment – the genuine, authentic you that doesn't carry around stress, shame, and criticism. The more you practice, the more you'll live with the last-row perspective by default
and be able to move back there whenever needed.

PSYCHOLOGY

The Psychology card delves into the depths of the mind, highlighting the importance of understanding your thoughts, emotions, and behaviors. It symbolizes self-awareness, introspection, and the exploration of your inner world. This card invites you to reflect on your psychological patterns, encouraging you to gain insights that lead to personal growth and healing.

Key Meanings:

Self-Awareness: Explore your thoughts, emotions, and behaviors with curiosity and honesty. By understanding yourself better, you can make more informed choices
and foster personal growth.

Introspection: Introspection is key to psychological understanding. Take time for self-reflection, examining your inner world without judgment. Introspection can reveal underlying patterns and motivations, helping you address and resolve internal conflicts.

Understanding Patterns: Identify recurring themes in your thoughts and behaviors, exploring how past experiences shape your present actions. By recognizing these patterns, you can break free from negative cycles and create healthier habits.

Healing and Growth: Psychological exploration often leads to healing and growth. Seek out therapeutic or self-help methods that support your mental and emotional well-being. Committing to your psychological health, whether through therapy, journaling, or mindfulness practices, fosters a more balanced and fulfilling life.

Takeaway:

Delve into your inner world and explore your psychological landscape. Engage in self-awareness and introspection, understanding your thoughts, emotions, and behaviors more deeply. Consider how you can identify and address psychological patterns that impact your life, seeking out methods of healing and growth. By prioritizing your psychological well-being, you pave the way for a more insightful, balanced, and empowered existence

Exercise:

Finding Patterns

Reflect on your thoughts and behaviors that come up regularly. Are these positive reflections of who you are? Do they serve the life you're leading and want to live into the future?

Think of patterns you have that you're not particularly proud of.

Perhaps its the way you react to challenges, a way you speak to loved ones when you are upset, or something you do when you are stressed.

The first step toward growth as a person is identifying where you can grow.

Identifying your patterns is a great place to start.

Once you've identified these patterns, you can start taking steps toward addressing them.

REALITY

The Reality card represents the importance of seeing things as they are, embracing the present moment, and grounding yourself in truth. It symbolizes the clarity and wisdom from facing facts and accepting the world without illusions or denial.

This card invites you to confront reality with courage and honesty, fostering a life built on a solid foundation of truth.

Key Meanings:

Facing Truth: Face the truth head-on about the external world and your inner self. Growth and progress begin with acknowledging facts, no matter how uncomfortable they might be. By confronting reality, you pave the way for genuine transformation.

Grounding in the Present: Reality involves being fully present and grounded in the here and now. Focus on the present moment rather than dwelling on the past or fantasizing about the future. Grounding yourself in the present allows you to deal with current situations effectively and with clear insight.

Acceptance and Clarity: Accept things as they are, letting go of illusions and wishful thinking. By embracing clarity, you better understand your circumstances and can make informed decisions that align with your true path.

Authenticity: Reality is about being authentic and true to yourself. Live in alignment with your values and beliefs without pretense or deceit. Embracing authenticity enhances your relationships, self-esteem, and overall sense of fulfillment.

Takeaway:

See things as they are and embrace the present moment with clarity and honesty. Confront illusions or denials, grounding yourself in truth and authenticity. Consider how you can better align with reality through accepting difficult truths, focusing on the present, or living more authentically. Doing so creates a foundation of truth that supports genuine growth and fulfillment.

Exercise:

Go with the Flow

This is an excellent exercise for getting into the present moment of reality.

I love swimming in the waves at the beach, but near my house, dangerous riptides (strong currents caused by tidal flow) sometimes suck swimmers out into deep water. Now, most people's instinct when caught in a riptide is to fight against it. But that just exhausts you and makes it harder to escape.

Instead of advising to fight against it, did you know that lifeguards teach swimmers to do just the opposite? When caught in a riptide, they say to just "go with the flow"–that is, just swim along with it. Soon, you'll come out of it with no trouble.

The same goes for the inner riptide called stress: If you feel stressed out, tense, uptight, nervous–anything at all–simply dive into your stress,
become aware of it, and you'll find you quickly come out of it.

If you let yourself go with the feeling, experience it, and even exaggerate it, an exciting thing happens. In minutes, the stress just vanishes. You'll feel energized, not exhausted, because you weren't fighting to get rid of the stress. Instead, you allowed the stress to sweep you along, and quickly, the stress just weakened and disappeared. Perhaps you'll hardly remember what it was. Soon, you'll be peacefully going about your day.

When you have enough awareness to experience stress and give up control, you gain even greater power while being present to this reality. Try this the next time you feel a stress riptide trying to pull your mind into a whirlwind of worry.

Go with the Flow in 5 Easy Steps

1. Become aware of your stress.
2. Stop fighting or trying to control it.
3. Feel it. Even exaggerate it!
4. Notice the stress ease up in minutes.
5. Become aware of your new state of mind.

RECEPTIVITY

The Receptivity card represents the art of being open to receive–whether it be ideas, opportunities, love, or guidance from the universe. It symbolizes the capacity to allow and accept without resistance, fostering openness and flow. This card invites you to embrace receptivity, encouraging you to soften your defenses and welcome life's abundance.

Key Meanings:

Openness to Receive: Life is filled with opportunities, love, and guidance waiting to flow into your experience. By cultivating an open and receptive mindset, you create space for these blessings to enter your life.

Letting Go of Resistance: Receptivity involves letting go of resistance and allowing things to unfold naturally. Release control and trust in the process. Embracing a state of surrender can lead to unexpected and wonderful outcomes.

Embracing Abundance: Embrace the abundance that is available to you. Recognize and accept the flow of prosperity, love, and opportunities. By affirming your worthiness and being open to abundance, you attract more positive experiences.

Intuition and Inner Guidance: Receptivity also involves attuning to your intuition and inner guidance. Listen to the subtle messages and insights that arise from within. Trusting your intuition can lead you towards paths aligned with your highest good.

Takeaway:

Open yourself to receive the blessings and guidance available to you.
Let go of resistance and control, embracing a flow state and allowing things to unfold naturally. Consider cultivating receptivity by being open to new ideas, opportunities, and love. By embracing receptivity, you create a welcoming space for abundance and positive experiences to enter your life.

Exercise:

Feel Your Aura

Sometimes, our receptivity allows us to pick up on the stress and negativity of others. Here's a technique that will help you stay relaxed and cheerful, no matter who or what is around you.

Imagine an aura around your body. An aura is a warm, glowing light just a few inches away from your body. It encloses your entire body like a soft, shining blanket that can comfort, relax, and protect you energetically.
Think of it as a force field that contains your positive, loving energy and keeps out unwanted negativity or stress. Only what you choose to let enter will pass through to you. You might think of this aura as made up of the radiant energy of everyone who has ever loved you, whether that be a parent, a spouse, your children, or even a pet. You can make your aura any color you wish or even a combination of colors.

Your aura relaxes away your stress by making you feel protected and secure. Every morning, keep your eyes closed and just feel your aura.
See it in your favorite color, all over your body, warming you and preparing you for the day.

Throughout the day, no matter what you're doing, notice your protective aura. You can do this while driving, shopping, at home, at work, or while doing nothing–just relax into it again and again.

When you carry your aura with you, your imagination will unify with your body and become a tremendously positive force against stress.

Feel Your Aura in 4 Easy Steps

1. Close your eyes and imagine your aura.
2. Feel its comfort, warmth, and protective love.
3. See it in your favorite color.
4. Imagine its protection around you as you continue your day.

RECIPROCITY

The Reciprocity card embodies the principle of mutual exchange and balance within relationships and interactions. It symbolizes the give-and-take dynamic that fosters harmony, trust, and equitable connections. This card invites you to reflect on the balance of giving and receiving in your life, emphasizing the importance of reciprocity in creating healthy and fulfilling relationships.

Key Meanings:

Balanced Exchange: Healthy connections are built on mutual giving and receiving. Ensuring a fair and balanced exchange of energy, support, and resources fosters
trust and harmony.

Mutual Respect: Reciprocity involves mutual respect and appreciation. Recognize and honor the contributions of others while also valuing your own. By appreciating what you give and receive, you cultivate relationships based on equality and respect.

Healthy Boundaries: Healthy boundaries are essential in maintaining balanced relationships. Set and respect boundaries, ensuring the exchange remains equitable and neither party feels depleted or taken advantage of.

Generosity and Gratitude: Reciprocity thrives on generosity and gratitude. Give freely and receive graciously, acknowledging the contributions of others with thankfulness. Cultivating an attitude of gratitude enhances positive energy flow and reinforces the principle of mutual exchange.

Takeaway:

Assess the balance of giving and receiving in your life. Reflect on your relationships and interactions, ensuring they are characterized by mutual respect, balanced exchange, and healthy boundaries. Consider how you can foster reciprocity by giving generously, receiving graciously, and appreciating the contributions of others. By embracing the principle of reciprocity, you create harmonious and fulfilling connections that support your well-being and growth.

Exercise:

Take a moment to consider your most important relationships. Are they balanced in giving and receiving? Are there any relationships where you could give more? Are there any relationships where you feel your efforts aren't being reciprocated? What can you do to enhance your relationships?

RELATIONSHIPS

The Relationships card represents the fundamental connections we form with others, reflecting our interactions, bonds, and mutual support systems. It symbolizes the importance of healthy, nurturing relationships and their role in our emotional and spiritual growth. This card invites you to reflect on your relationships and foster those that bring joy, support, and growth.

Key Meanings:

Connection and Bonding: Form and nurture connections with others. Relationships provide a sense of belonging and support. Building strong bonds with family, friends, and partners enriches your life and fosters a sense of community.

Mutual Support: Healthy relationships are built on mutual support and understanding. Both give and receive support within your relationships. Acts of kindness, active listening, and empathy strengthen your connections and create a foundation of trust and respect.

Communication and Understanding: Effective communication that is open, honest, and respectful is crucial in maintaining healthy relationships. Expressing your thoughts and feelings clearly and listening to others with an open heart can resolve conflicts and deepen your connections.

Growth and Nurturing: Relationships are opportunities for personal and mutual growth. Nurture your relationships by investing time, energy, and love. Recognize the potential for growth within each connection, allowing yourself and others to evolve and flourish together.

Takeaway:

Reflect on and nurture your connections with others. Assess the health of your relationships and invest in those that bring joy, support, and growth. Consider improving communication, offering and receiving support, and nurturing your bonds. You create a strong support system and enhance your emotional and spiritual well-being by fostering healthy relationships.

Exercise:

Create a Better Relationship with Yourself

To have better relationships with others, you must nourish your relationship with yourself, including your body! As the saying goes:
You cannot give from an empty cup.

First, remember: This is the body you have that's been with you all these years and will be with you the rest of your life. And it's a beautiful and complex instrument. It functions beautifully and silently for many years–whether you're asleep or awake.

Without much care, even with some neglect, it keeps on running. Even when your body is not feeling well or has a problem, it's always working for you, always trying its best.

Decide that you're done ignoring it. Commit to yourself right now. Your body is listening. Start loving your body, caring for it, and listening to it, too. Remember, all healthy relationships are reciprocal.

Make friends with your body. Build a relationship with it.

Create a Better Relationship with Your Body in 4 Easy Steps

1. Acknowledge your body and how well it has functioned for you.
2. Love, care and listen to it.
3. What does your body need? Rest? Good food? Movement? Water? Sleep?
4. Take time daily to check in with your body and give it what it needs?

RELAXATION

The Relaxation card symbolizes the essential act of unwinding, letting go, and allowing yourself to experience moments of calm and tranquility. It represents the need to step back from the hustle and bustle of daily life and prioritize rest and rejuvenation. This card invites you to embrace relaxation as a vital aspect of your
well-being, fostering balance and inner peace.

Key Meanings:

Prioritize Rest: Make time for rest and relaxation in your daily routine. Relaxation is not a luxury but a necessity for maintaining your overall health and well-being.
By prioritizing rest, you allow your body and mind to recover and rejuvenate.

Letting Go of Stress: Relaxation involves releasing stress and tension. Identify sources of stress in your life and actively seek ways to let go of them. Whether through deep breathing exercises, meditation, or simply taking a break from your responsibilities, finding ways to relax can significantly improve your mental and emotional state.

Creating a Peaceful Environment: Cultivate spaces that promote relaxation, whether it's a quiet corner in your home, a serene outdoor spot, or even a mental sanctuary through visualization techniques. A peaceful environment supports your ability to unwind and find inner calm.

Self-Care and Renewal: Relaxation is a key component of self-care and renewal. Engage in activities that bring you joy and relaxation, such as reading a good book, taking a walk in nature, or enjoying a hobby. By regularly engaging in relaxing activities, you nurture your spirit and enhance your overall well-being.

Takeaway:

Make time for rest and prioritize relaxation in your life. Identify and release sources of stress, creating a peaceful environment that supports your need for tranquility. Consider how you can incorporate more relaxation into your daily routine and engage in self-care practices that renew and rejuvenate you. By embracing relaxation, you can achieve greater balance, inner peace, and overall well-being.

Exercise:

Breathing Colors

Focus on your breathing and notice your turning points: inhale-*turn (pause)*, exhale-*turn (pause)*. This time, as you're watching yourself breathe, switch the experience into Technicolor.

For example, if you find that purple is a restful, relaxing color, imagine breathing in purple and letting it circulate and move everywhere in your body from head to toe. Then, exhale purple as you release your tension and stress. Then, try bright orange! Breathe it in, let it go everywhere inside and absorb your tension, then breathe it out.

Get playful with this and use the colors you love. Maybe blue for tranquility and peace. Green for groundedness and presence. Just continue to observe your breathing, letting the color circulate and move everywhere inside, then exhale the color, and with it, your stress.

Breathing Colors in 5 Easy Steps

1. Become aware of your breathing.
2. Switch your breathing into Technicolor.
3. Breathe in a color of your choosing and visualize it circulating in your body as you inhale.
4. Imagine the color absorbing your stress and leaving your body on the exhale.
5. Repeat steps 2 - 4 with as many colors as you'd like!

RESOLUTION

The Resolution card signifies the process of finding solutions, closure, and clarity in challenging or unresolved situations. It symbolizes the end of conflicts, the achievement of understanding, and the restoration of peace. This card invites you to seek resolution in your life, encouraging you to address lingering issues and embrace the calm that follows.

Key Meanings:

Finding Solutions: Resolution often requires creativity, patience, and a willingness to see different perspectives. You can bring about positive change and harmony by seeking out and implementing solutions.

Achieving Closure: Resolution involves resolving past issues and moving forward.
Let go of unresolved matters that may be weighing you down. You can find peace and create space for new beginnings by addressing these issues directly.

Restoring Peace: Seek harmony in your relationships and environments. Fostering peace is crucial in the resolution process, whether through mediation, forgiveness, or open communication.

Clarity and Understanding: Resolution brings clarity and understanding to previously confusing or contentious situations. Seek the truth and be open to new insights that can lead to resolution. You can make informed decisions and confidently move forward by gaining a clear understanding.

Takeaway:

Seek out and embrace solutions to any unresolved issues in your life.
Find closure and restore peace, whether in personal relationships, work situations, or within yourself. Consider how you can address lingering conflicts or misunderstandings and take steps to resolve them.
Doing so can achieve clarity, understanding, and a sense of harmony.

Exercise:

Journaling Brainstorm

Reflect on a challenging or unresolved situation in your life.
Ask yourself, "What is a different perspective on this?" Write about that different perspective in detail. If it was someone else looking at the same situation, what would they say? How would they feel? What might they suggest you do for the next step?

SELF-ACCEPTANCE

The Self-Acceptance card embodies the profound act of embracing yourself fully, including your strengths, weaknesses, and everything in between. It symbolizes the journey towards loving and accepting yourself unconditionally, recognizing your inherent worth without judgment. This card invites you to cultivate deep self-acceptance, fostering inner peace and genuine self-love.

Key Meanings:

Embracing Your True Self: Self-acceptance begins with acknowledging and honoring all parts of yourself, including your imperfections and vulnerabilities. By accepting yourself as you are, you create a foundation for genuine self-love and inner peace.

Letting Go of Judgment: Self-acceptance involves letting go of self-judgment and critical inner voices. Release harsh judgments and unrealistic expectations you may hold about yourself. Practicing self-compassion and forgiveness allows you to see yourself through a lens of love and understanding.

Acknowledging Inherent Worth: See beyond societal standards and external validations, understanding that your worth is intrinsic and not dependent on your achievements or appearance.

Fostering Inner Peace: Self-acceptance is a path to inner peace and emotional well-being. Cultivate practices that nurture self-acceptance, such as mindfulness, positive affirmations, or therapy. By fostering self-acceptance, you create a harmonious relationship with yourself, leading to greater overall happiness and fulfillment.

Takeaway:

Embrace and accept yourself fully. Practice self-compassion, letting go of judgment, and recognizing your inherent worth. Consider how you can nurture a loving and accepting relationship with yourself, acknowledging all parts of your being. By cultivating self-acceptance, you pave the way for inner peace, self-love, and a more fulfilling life.

Exercise:

Create a New Relationship with Your Body

Privately, stand in your underwear (nude is even better), and look at your body in front of a full-length mirror. (If you can't do this physically, imagine it.) Be aware of your feelings and any thoughts that come up.

First, step up to the mirror so close that you're almost touching the glass.
Notice that your head, nose, and eyes are large and out of proportion. You can hardly even see your body. You likely feel grotesque and ugly–it's a
hall of mirrors experience–and you can easily reject this image.

Next, take a step back; you can see your whole body now, but you're so close to the image that it's easy to pick out your body's flaws and exaggerate them–and then judge and criticize yourself.

Finally, step even further back–say about ten feet back–and now you can see the complete picture of yourself. You're a human being with a unique body, spirit, energy, warmth, and style. Just remember: Each of these three images in the mirror is you. It's simply a matter of having a different perspective, seeing things with different eyes, and seeing the bigger picture.

Do this exercise for one minute every morning and one minute every night.
The benefits are extraordinary. Within a few days, you'll find a new and more positive body image. Plus, you'll become more accepting of your whole self, which will then help you grow in self-confidence and self-respect.

Your willingness to see and accept yourself as you are will also work wonders in all your relationships. When you're more comfortable with yourself, you're more comfortable with others. When you laugh at yourself, you can laugh more easily with your friends. And only when you love yourself can you truly love another person.

Create a New Relationship with Your Body in 6 Easy Steps

1. Look at your nude body in a full-length mirror.
   Allow yourself to feel whatever comes up.
2. Step up close to the mirror, noticing your warped perspective.
3. Step far away from the mirror and see the complete picture of yourself.
4. Notice your change in perspective and how that impacts your self-image.
5. Repeat daily and note how you feel.

SELF-RESPECT

The Self-Respect card represents the importance of valuing yourself, setting healthy boundaries, and maintaining a strong sense of personal integrity. It symbolizes honoring your worth and standing up for your needs and beliefs. This card invites you to cultivate self-respect by acknowledging your inherent dignity and ensuring that your actions and choices reflect this respect.

Key Meanings:

Valuing Yourself: Recognize and value your inherent worth. Self-respect begins with acknowledging your dignity and treating yourself with kindness and compassion. You set the foundation for how others will treat you by valuing yourself.

Setting Boundaries: Self-respect involves setting and maintaining healthy boundaries. Clearly define your limits and communicate them assertively. Boundaries protect your well-being and ensure your relationships and interactions honor your needs and values.

Personal Integrity: Live in alignment with your values and beliefs. Act with integrity, make choices that reflect your principles and stay true to yourself. Upholding your personal integrity fosters a sense of self-trust and authenticity.

Standing Up for Yourself: Self-respect requires the courage to stand up for yourself and assert your needs and rights. Speak up and advocate for yourself when your boundaries or values are challenged. By asserting yourself respectfully, you reinforce your self-worth and command respect from others.

Takeaway:

Honor and value yourself. Cultivate self-respect by recognizing your worth, setting healthy boundaries, and acting with integrity. Consider how you can respectfully and assertively assert your needs
and stand up for your beliefs. Embracing self-respect creates a foundation for healthier relationships and a more authentic and fulfilling life.

Exercise:

Create a New Relationship with Your Body

Privately, stand in your underwear (nude is even better), and look at your body in front of a full-length mirror. (If you can't do this physically, imagine it.) Be aware of your feelings. Perhaps you'll like some parts of what you see more than others. Most people find some features difficult and unacceptable because they're frustrated or dissatisfied with them.

Perhaps you see plumpness in your face. Maybe you hate your stomach or your hips so much you can barely stand to look at them. Maybe you see signs of obesity and can't bear to stay connected with the thoughts and feelings these signs evoke.

For most, the reaction is to escape–to repress feelings, judge, reject, deny, disown, and try not to be parts of yourself.

Rather than look away, try to stay focused on your body for just a few more minutes. Keep looking in the mirror, take some deep breaths,
and repeat to yourself these two sentences:

1. "I accept that I am judging my body and myself. I accept that I'm judging because I know that judging myself for being judgmental is the #1 reason I [stress/overeat/engage in unhealthy habits/etc.].
2. "I accept my body as it is. I am 100% friendly, caring and compassionate towards my body. I respect myself."

Create a New Relationship with Your Body in 2 Easy Steps

1. Look at your nude body in a full-length mirror.
   Allow yourself to feel whatever comes up.
2. Lovingly say the above prompts to yourself through the mirror.

SENSES OPEN

The Senses Open card symbolizes fully engaging with the world through your senses, heightening your awareness and presence. It represents the richness of experiences from being attuned to your surroundings and inner sensations. This card invites you to embrace the full spectrum of sensory experiences, enhancing your connection to the present moment and deepening your appreciation of life.

Key Meanings:

Heightened Awareness: Heightened awareness supports better mindfulness. Fully engage with your surroundings, paying attention to the details and nuances of what you see, hear, smell, taste, and touch. Doing so enriches your experience and deepens your connection to the present moment.

Mindfulness and Presence: Engaging your senses is a powerful way to cultivate mindfulness and presence. Anchor yourself in the now by immersing yourself in sensory experiences. Whether it's savoring a meal, listening to music, or feeling the textures around you, these practices help you stay grounded and aware.

Enhanced Perception: You can gain new insights and perspectives by attuning to your senses. This heightened sensitivity can lead to greater creativity, intuition, and appreciation for the beauty and complexity of the world.

Joy and Appreciation: Fully engaging your senses can bring immense joy and appreciation. Celebrate life's sensory pleasures, from the sun's warmth on your skin to the fragrance of flowers in bloom. By appreciating these moments, you cultivate a sense of gratitude and fulfillment.

Takeaway:

Immerse yourself in sensory experiences and heighten your awareness. Practice mindfulness by engaging fully with your senses, enhancing your presence and perception. Consider how you can bring more sensory richness into your daily life, whether through nature walks, art, music, or simply savoring everyday moments. Keeping your senses open can deepen your connection to the present and enrich your life with joy and appreciation.

Exercise:

Tune Into Your Senses

Whenever you feel stressed and uptight, caught up in difficult thoughts and feelings, take a moment to visit your favorite place and let yourself relax in the simple pleasure of your five senses.

Tune Into Your Senses in 7 Easy Steps

1. Take a few deep let-go breaths.
2. Go to your favorite place.
3. Be your eyes and see this place in detail.
4. Be your ears and hear this place in detail.
5. Be your nose and smell this place in detail.
6. Be your tongue and taste this place in detail.
7. Be your touch and feel this place in detail.

SEXUALITY

The Sexuality card represents the vital, dynamic energy of sexual expression and the profound connection between body, mind, and spirit. It symbolizes the acceptance and celebration of your sexual identity and the healthy exploration of desire and intimacy. This card invites you to embrace your sexuality as a natural and empowering aspect of your being, fostering deeper connections with yourself and others.

Key Meanings:

Embrace Your Sexuality: Embrace your sexual identity and desires without shame or judgment. Sexuality is a natural and integral part of who you are. By accepting and celebrating your sexuality, you can experience greater confidence and self-love.

Healthy Exploration: Sexuality involves the healthy exploration of your desires and boundaries. Explore your sexual preferences and fantasies in a safe and consensual manner. Understanding and communicating your needs and boundaries can lead to more fulfilling and respectful intimate relationships.

Connection and Intimacy: Sexuality is a powerful avenue for connection and intimacy. By fostering open and honest communication with your partner(s), you can deepen your connections and enhance the quality of your intimate experiences.

Healing and Empowerment: Healing and empowerment can come from embracing your sexual self. Heal any past wounds or traumas related to sexuality and reclaim your sexual power. Doing so can transform negative experiences into sources of strength and empowerment.

Takeaway:

Embrace and celebrate your sexual identity and desires. Explore your sexuality in a healthy and consensual way, fostering deeper connections and intimacy in your relationships. Recognize the importance of open communication, consent, and mutual respect in intimate interactions. By accepting and honoring your sexuality, you can experience greater confidence, healing, and empowerment.

Exercise:

Affirmations

Create a list of positive affirmations about your sexuality. Examples might include: "My sexuality is a natural and beautiful part of me," "I celebrate my desires and express them freely," or "I am worthy of love and deep connection.

SIGNALS (MIND-BODY)

The Mind-Body Signals card represents the intrinsic connection between your mental and physical states, highlighting the importance of listening to your body's messages. It symbolizes the wisdom and guidance gained from tuning into these signals, fostering holistic well-being. This card invites you to develop a greater awareness of your mind-body connection, using it as a tool for self-care and healing.

Key Meanings:

Listening to Your Body: Pay attention to the messages your body communicates. Physical sensations, emotions, and even ailments often reveal your overall well-being. Tuning into these signals can address underlying issues and promote healing.

Holistic Awareness: Understanding mind-body signals involves cultivating holistic awareness. Consider how your thoughts, emotions, and physical sensations are interconnected. Recognizing patterns and correlations between your mental and physical states can lead to greater self-awareness and balance.

Self-Care and Healing: Take proactive steps to nurture your well-being, whether through rest, exercise, nutrition, or mindfulness practices. Prioritizing self-care helps you respond to your body's needs and supports healing and vitality.

Emotional and Physical Balance: Mind-body signals often indicate areas where you need more balance. Explore ways to harmonize your emotional and physical states. Practices such as meditation, yoga, or journaling can help you achieve a balanced and integrated sense of well-being.

Takeaway:

Listen closely to the messages your body is sending you. Develop a greater awareness of the connection between your mind and body, using this awareness to guide your self-care and healing practices. Consider how your physical sensations, emotions, and thoughts are interrelated, and take steps to address any imbalances. Tuning into your mind-body signals can help you achieve a more harmonious and healthy state of being.

Exercise:

Body Signals Understood

One of the loudest messages your body can send you is a feeling of pain or discomfort. This pain could be a persistent headache, hypertension, digestive disorders, decreased sex drive, muscle tension, and much more.

First, close your eyes and focus on an area of your body where you're hurting; or if you're feeling good today, focus on a place where you usually feel discomfort. We all have parts of our body that bother us–the lower back, the knee, the shoulder, the neck–you know where you usually hurt. Wherever your discomfort happens, place one of your hands directly on that spot and say these words aloud but softly: "Please relax, please relax, please relax."

It also helps to caress your stress. With your hand on the area of discomfort, and as you're saying, "Please relax," go ahead and, with very light pressure, rub the site with your fingertips in a counter-clockwise motion. Start in the very center of the area and circle out wider and wider. Talk to your body while you unwind your discomfort gently with your fingertips.

Whenever you do this technique, you're taking the time to get in touch with your body and care for yourself gently and compassionately.

Body Signals Understood in 5 Easy Steps

1. Close your eyes and bring your focus to an area of pain or where you
   usually feel discomfort.
2. Place one hand on the area and say softly, "Please relax," three times.
3. Caress the area as you gently request your body to relax.
4. Rub the area in counter-clockwise circles and with light pressure, circling outwards.
5. Talk to your body gently, listening for a response or acknowledging a shift.

SLEEP

The Sleep card embodies the restorative power of rest and its essential role in maintaining physical, mental, and emotional well-being. It symbolizes the importance of taking time to recharge, heal, and rejuvenate. This card invites you to honor your need for sleep and rest, recognizing it as a fundamental aspect of self-care and overall health.

Key Meanings:

Rest and Rejuvenation: Rest and the rejuvenation it brings are necessary. Adequate sleep is crucial for physical health, mental clarity, and emotional balance. You allow your body and mind to heal and recharge by prioritizing restful sleep.

Self-Care: Sleep is a fundamental component of self-care. Recognize the value of sleep in your daily routine. Making sleep a priority reflects a commitment to your overall well-being, enabling you to function at your best and maintain a healthy, balanced life.

Healing and Recovery: Healing and recovery occur during sleep. Embrace sleep as a time for your body to repair itself, your mind to process emotions and experiences, and your spirit to find peace and solace. Quality sleep supports healing on all levels.

Dreams and Intuition: Sleep is also a gateway to the subconscious mind and the realm of dreams. Pay attention to your dreams, as they can provide valuable insights and intuitive guidance. Embrace the messages and symbols that emerge from your dreams, using them as tools for self-discovery and spiritual growth.

Takeaway:

Prioritize rest and rejuvenation in your life. Honor your need for sleep, recognizing its critical role in maintaining your health and well-being.
Consider the quality and quantity of your sleep, and create a restful environment and routine. Pay attention to your dreams and their insights, and embrace sleep as a time for healing, recovery, and intuitive exploration.

Exercise:

Beauty Sleep Technique

Getting a great night's sleep is important for health, wellness, focus, and positivity. The Beauty Sleep technique is for less stress, less overthinking, and less self-doubt. It helps increase the success of all the other techniques because your mindset will be rested, calm, strong,
and primed for growth and improvement.

The Beauty Sleep technique requires about 5-15 minutes and will turn your sleep into a valuable meditation and mindfulness practice.

Count from 0 to 100, then 100 to 0, counting inhales only. Inhale and say "zero" to yourself and not out loud. Exhale easily. With the next breath, inhale and say "one." Exhale. Continue this with your inhales and count from zero to one hundred. If you lose track of the numbers, always go back to zero and start all over. You may fall asleep before you get to one hundred. If you get to one hundred, count your inhales only from one hundred to zero. You can do this 1, 2, or 3 times.

And here's another thing: Have you ever noticed that your last thought at night will be your first thought in the morning? Most people go to sleep focusing on the past or dwelling on mistakes. Observe this thought when you enter sleep, and try to make that last thought one of mind-body healing instead. That way, the intention will remain like a beautiful fragrance around you all night. It will fill your inner space, and in the morning when you awake, it'll be there. Naturally, in the morning,
after eight hours of mind-body healing meditation, you will have a happier, more relaxed, positive energy, inside and out.

Sweet dreams!

The Beauty Sleep Technique in 4 Easy Steps

1. As you fall asleep, think positive thoughts of rest and healing.
2. Count from 0 to 100, then 100 to 0, counting inhales only.
3. If you lose track of the numbers, always go back to zero and start all over.
4. Do this 1, 2 or 3 times.

SPIRITUALITY

The Spirituality card embodies the essence of your connection to the divine, the universe, and your inner self. It symbolizes the quest for deeper meaning, inner peace, and enlightenment. This card invites you to explore and nurture your spiritual path, seeking a harmonious balance between your physical existence and your spiritual aspirations.

Key Meanings:

Connection to the Divine: Consider your connection to a higher power, whether the divine, the universe, or your inner self. Strengthen this connection through practices such as prayer, meditation, or contemplation. Fostering a deeper spiritual connection can help you find guidance, comfort, and inspiration daily.

Inner Peace and Enlightenment: Spirituality is often associated with the pursuit of inner peace and enlightenment. Seek tranquility and clarity within yourself. Through spiritual practices, you can achieve a state of inner calm and gain a greater understanding of your purpose and existence.

Exploration and Growth: Spiritual exploration is an ongoing journey. Be open to new experiences, teachings, and perspectives that enhance your spiritual understanding. Embrace the journey with curiosity and a willingness to learn and evolve.

Harmony and Balance: Spirituality involves finding harmony and balance between your physical and spiritual lives. Integrate your spiritual beliefs and practices into your everyday life, creating a balanced and holistic approach to living. You can achieve a more fulfilling and harmonious existence by aligning your actions with your spiritual values

Takeaway:

Nurture your spiritual journey and deepen your connection to the divine. Seek inner peace, explore new spiritual teachings, and find harmony between your physical and spiritual lives. Recognize the importance of your spiritual well-being and make time for practices that foster growth and enlightenment. By embracing your spiritual path, you can better understand yourself and the universe, leading to a more fulfilling and purposeful life.

Exercise:

Reflect on the divine within yourself: take a few moments each day to meditate and connect with your higher self, feeling the presence of inner peace and wisdom. As you do, write down any insights or messages you receive, trusting that they are guiding you toward your spiritual path.

STRENGTH

The Strength card symbolizes inner power, resilience, and overcoming challenges with grace and determination. It represents the courage to face adversity,
the patience to endure trials, and the fortitude to remain steadfast in pursuing your goals. This card invites you to connect with your inner strength, trust in your abilities, and navigate life's obstacles with confidence and compassion.

Key Meanings:

Inner Power: You possess the strength to overcome any challenges that come your way. You can face difficulties with confidence and poise by tapping into your
inner resources.

Courage and Determination: Strength involves the courage to confront fears and the determination to persevere despite obstacles. Be brave and steadfast in the pursuit of your goals. True strength comes from facing adversity with a positive and determined mindset.

Patience and Compassion: Approach challenges with a gentle and understanding attitude. Combining strength with kindness creates a powerful force for overcoming difficulties and fostering growth.

Endurance and Stability: Strength is about enduring hardships and maintaining stability in the face of change. Build a solid foundation that supports you through tough times. You can navigate life's ups and downs with resilience and grace by staying grounded and focused.

Takeaway:

Connect with your inner power and resilience. Approach challenges with courage, determination, and patience. Recognize the strength within you, and trust in your ability to overcome any obstacles. Embrace the qualities of compassion and kindness, both for yourself and others, as you navigate through life's difficulties. By tapping into your inner strength and remaining steadfast, you can achieve your goals and emerge stronger from any experience.

Exercise:

Footwork

To start, turn your attention to your feet and focus your weight and energy on them. When we shift our weight lower and focus on the heaviness of our feet, we feel strong and stable.

If you've ever played a sport, you may have been told to "keep your weight low." That's because lowering your center of gravity is the foundation of your balance and power.

So, any time you want to feel your inner strength, just focus on the weight of your feet.

Footwork in 3 Easy Steps

1. Turn your attention to your feet.
2. Focus your weight and energy on your feet.
3. Notice a change in the way you feel.

SUBCONSCIOUS

The Subconscious card represents the hidden depths of your mind, where memories, instincts, and untapped potential reside. It symbolizes the powerful, yet often unnoticed, influence of your inner world on your thoughts, emotions, and behaviors. This card invites you to explore the mysteries of your subconscious, bringing awareness to the aspects of yourself that shape your reality and unlocking the potential for profound personal transformation.

Key Meanings:

Hidden Influences: Hidden influences shape your thoughts, emotions, and actions. Much of what drives you lies beneath the surface of conscious awareness. By exploring these hidden aspects, you can gain insight into your motivations and desires.

Inner Exploration: Delve into the recesses of your mind, uncovering buried memories, suppressed emotions, and latent potential. You can access the wisdom and insights held within your subconscious through meditation, journaling, or hypnosis.

Healing and Integration: Heal and integrate the hidden aspects of yourself. Confront and embrace your shadow side–the parts of yourself that you may have repressed or denied. By acknowledging and integrating these aspects, you achieve greater wholeness and self-acceptance.

Intuition: Pay attention to your dreams, gut feelings, and the symbolic messages in your life. These intuitive insights can guide you toward more profound understanding and personal growth.

Takeaway:

Explore the hidden depths of your mind and bring awareness to the subconscious forces in your life. Engage in practices that foster introspection and self-discovery, allowing you to uncover and heal buried emotions and patterns. Trust your intuition and pay attention to the symbols and messages from your subconscious mind. By embracing the mysteries of your inner world, you can achieve profound transformation and self-awareness.

Exercise:

Going to the Movies

Start by imagining a movie theater. Visualize all the theater details – the smell of popcorn, the red velvet curtains, the dim lighting, the comfortable seats – maybe it's an IMAX theater or one with reclining seats! You enter the theater, choose your seat, get settled, and the movie has already started. But this time, the movie on the big screen is all about you.

You're the star, and it's your story. It's your work life, home life, performance, and how you deal with people, demands, success, and failure. It's a movie about your whole life.

Sitting in the 15th row – right in the middle of the theater – is your Inner Critic. This is the judgmental, controlling, never satisfied part of you. We all have this Inner Critic watching our movie, ready to tell us everything that's wrong with us.

But there's another "you" in the theater, too, sitting quietly in the last row of the theater: your Last Row Self. Your Last Row Self is your wisdom, creativity, and freedom. It's the "you" when you feel calm and peaceful, and where you can look at your movie, and at your Inner Critic in the 15th row, with understanding and love.

The Three Perspectives When You Go to the Movies

1.) You as the Star of the Movie: working, playing, driving, shopping, dealing with bosses, raising kids, keeping schedules, and feeling pushed, hurried, and stressed.
2.) Your Inner Critic in the 15th row: ready to find fault and punish you for your mistakes. The part of you that gets stuck in stress.
3.) The Last Row: the friendly, caring, and compassionate part of you that loves yourself just as you are, including your Inner Critic.

Going to the Movies in Three Steps

Now that you know the concept of "Going to the Movies" and can visualize your inner theater, it's time to practice. Whenever you feel upset, tense, or stressed out, do these three steps in order:

Step 1 - Be in your movie. Be present in the moment and experience what's happening in your movie. Let the scene unfold; feel yourself acting your role. After all, you're the star! Let yourself express your stress: "I'm in trouble.... I'm way behind, and there's no way I can catch up!" "I'm going to be late!" "How am I going to make this month's payment?" Let yourself think and feel everything that's going on in the scene.

Step 2 - Now, move your awareness to the 15th row. Let your Inner Critic criticize the scene. From the 15th row, focus on what's wrong with you and your thoughts and feelings: "Stop whining and get to work." "You should've started earlier." "Why did you buy it in the first place?" Let your Inner Critic be hostile and have its say.

Step 3 - Get up and walk back to the last row of the theater. Visualize yourself getting up and physically moving. There, in the last row, watch your movie and your 15th-row Inner Critic with detachment. Become aware and accept your breathing to help transport yourself to the last-row perspective–free, calm, peaceful, relaxed, observant, comfortable with yourself, friendly, caring, and compassionate.

Keep coming back to this technique. Going to the last row is coming home to YOU in the present moment – the genuine, authentic you that doesn't carry around stress, shame, and criticism. The more you practice, the more you'll live with the last-row perspective by default and be able to move back there whenever needed.

SUCCESS

The Success card symbolizes achievement, fulfillment, and the realization of goals and aspirations. It represents the culmination of hard work, dedication, and perseverance. This card invites you to recognize and celebrate your accomplishments, both big and small, and to understand that true success is not only about external achievements but also about inner satisfaction and growth.

Key Meanings:

Achievement and Recognition: Acknowledge and celebrate your accomplishments, no matter how significant or modest they may be. Recognizing your success fosters a positive mindset and motivates you to pursue further goals.

Hard Work and Perseverance: Success is often the result of sustained effort and perseverance. Appreciate the hard work and dedication that brought you to this point. Persistence and resilience are key components of achieving your goals.

Inner Fulfillment: True success encompasses both external achievements and inner fulfillment. Reflect on what success means to you personally, beyond societal expectations or material rewards. Inner fulfillment comes from pursuing your passions, living authentically, and finding joy in the journey.

Continuous Growth: Each success is a stepping stone to greater accomplishments and deeper understanding. Embrace the process of continuous learning and improvement, recognizing that success is a dynamic and evolving concept.

Takeaway:

Celebrate your achievements and recognize the hard work and dedication that have brought you this far. Reflect on the true meaning of success in your life, considering both external accomplishments and inner fulfillment. Acknowledge the importance of perseverance and resilience, and embrace the ongoing journey of growth and development. By celebrating your successes and staying motivated,
you continue to pave the way for future achievements and personal fulfillment.

Exercise:

The definition of success is subjective. Journal about what success means to you. What does it look and feel like, in detail? What achievements, goals and aspirations will have been fulfilled? What will you have to do to get there?

SUPPRESSION

The Suppression card represents burying emotions, thoughts, or desires deep within, often out of fear, shame, or a desire to conform. It symbolizes the internal pressures and emotional burdens that accumulate when we deny or repress parts of ourselves. This card invites you to confront and release what you have suppressed, allowing for healing, self-expression, and freedom.

Key Meanings:

Repressed Emotions: Examine the emotions you have buried within yourself. Unexpressed feelings can lead to emotional and physical distress. By acknowledging and releasing these emotions, you can begin to heal and restore balance to your life.

Internal Pressure: Suppression creates internal pressure and tension, which can manifest as stress, anxiety, or physical ailments. Recognize the areas of your life where you feel constricted or burdened. Addressing these pressures can alleviate the weight on your mind and body.

Fear of Expression: Do you fear expressing your true self? You may hold back parts of yourself due to fear of judgment, rejection, or conflict. Find safe and healthy ways to express your thoughts, feelings, and desires.

Path to Liberation: Suppression is a barrier to freedom and authenticity. Embark on a path of self-liberation, confronting and releasing what you have kept hidden. You achieve a greater sense of wholeness and freedom by embracing your true self and allowing your suppressed parts to surface.

Takeaway:

Confront and release what you have been holding back. Identify and acknowledge your suppressed emotions, thoughts, and desires, and find healthy outlets for their expression. Recognize your internal pressures and burdens, and take steps to alleviate them. By embracing your true self and allowing suppressed aspects to surface, you pave the way for healing, authenticity, and liberation.

Exercise:

Clear the Air

Emotional repression– denying your feelings, holding them in, pushing them down in your body–creates a dangerous kind of stress in your life.
It's like having a large spring in your chest, and when you deny your feelings, you're pressing the spring down, compressing it, and feeling all
the pressure and tension mounting, waiting to uncoil.

Take a couple of deep, let-go breaths, really pushing your exhales. Now, eyes open or closed, imagine all of your stress issues–all your worries and frustrations, all your worst memories, your family problems, guilts, jealousies, resentments–imagine all this packed tightly into a small, stuffy, stale-smelling room. The smell is so sour and stifling you can barely breathe. Now, picture yourself throwing open a window. Clear and sweet, fresh breeze blows in, and all your stress swirls and drifts outside, floating up and dispersing into thin air. Take three deep, satisfying breaths and relax.

You can also do this in your car when you're on the go for daily stress issues. Let's say you're driving home from a stressful day at work. Let all your feelings–maybe anger, frustration, or worry–fill the car and foul the air; then just open your car window and watch as your stress swirls out and floats away.

Clear the Air in 6 Easy Steps

1. Take a couple of deep, let-go breaths. Push the exhales.
2. Imagine your stress stuffed into a small, smelly room.
3. Feel the stifling sour odor; you can hardly take it!
4. Picture yourself throwing open a window and allowing in a sweet,
   clearing breeze.
5. Watch your stresses drift out of the window and disperse.
6. Take three deep, satisfying breaths.

TANTRA

The Tantra card embodies the profound connection between the physical and spiritual, the sacred and the sensual. It symbolizes the integration of all aspects of existence and invites you to explore the deep, transformative power of unity and balance. This card encourages you to embrace the full spectrum of your being, recognizing that true spiritual growth involves honoring and harmonizing both
the physical and the spiritual dimensions of life.

Key Meanings:

Integration of Body and Spirit: Integrate the physical and spiritual aspects of your being. True wholeness comes from honoring both your bodily desires and spiritual aspirations. By embracing and balancing these dimensions, you cultivate a deeper sense of fulfillment and harmony.

Sacred Sexuality: Tantra emphasizes the sacredness of sexuality and the profound spiritual potential of intimate connections. Explore your sexuality with mindfulness and reverence, recognizing it as a pathway to deeper intimacy, connection,
and spiritual growth. By approaching your sexual experiences as sacred, you open yourself to transformative healing and unity.

Union and Balance: There is a union and balance of opposing forces within and around you. Seek harmony between the masculine and feminine energies, the active and receptive, the light and shadow. By embracing and integrating these polarities, you create a state of equilibrium and inner peace.

Deep Connection: Tantra is about experiencing deep connection and oneness with yourself, others, and the universe. Cultivate meaningful relationships and connections that transcend the superficial, fostering a sense of unity and interconnectedness. By engaging in practices that deepen your connections, such as meditation, mindful touch, and conscious communication, you enhance your sense of belonging and spiritual growth.

Takeaway:

Embrace the sacredness of both your physical and spiritual experiences. Integrate all aspects of your being, honoring the unity and balance between body and spirit. Explore the depths of your connections, approach your sexuality with reverence, and seek harmony in all areas of your life. By embracing the principles of tantra, you open yourself to profound transformation, healing, and spiritual awakening.

Exercise:

Affirmation:

"I honor the sacred union of body, mind, and spirit within myself and with others. Through mindful presence and deep connection, I embrace the divine energy of tantra, cultivating love, passion, and spiritual growth in every intimate encounter."

TRUTHFUL

The Truthful card embodies the essence of honesty, integrity, and authenticity. It symbolizes the importance of living in alignment with your true self, speaking your truth, and upholding the principles of transparency and sincerity in all your interactions. This card invites you to embrace the power of truth, both within
yourself and in your relationships, as a foundation for trust, growth, and meaningful connections.

Key Meanings:

Self-Honesty: Be honest with yourself about your feelings, desires, and intentions. Self-honesty is the foundation of personal growth and self-acceptance. By acknowledging your true thoughts and emotions, you create a path to greater understanding and authenticity.

Authentic Expression: Truthfulness involves expressing your true self openly and sincerely. Communicate your thoughts and feelings with clarity and honesty, even when it feels challenging. Authentic expression fosters deeper connections and builds trust in your relationships.

Integrity: Integrity is important, so align your actions with your values and principles. Act with honesty and fairness in all situations. By living with integrity, you create a life of authenticity and respect, earning the trust and admiration of others.

Courage to Face the Truth: Embracing truthfulness requires courage to face difficult truths and confront falsehoods, both within yourself and in the world around you. The truth, while sometimes uncomfortable, is ultimately liberating and transformative. By facing the truth with courage, you pave the way for healing and growth.

Takeaway:

Embrace honesty, integrity, and authenticity in all areas of your life. Be honest with yourself about your true feelings and desires, communicate openly and sincerely with others, and act in alignment with your values. By living truthfully, you build a foundation of trust and respect, fostering deeper connections and personal growth.

Exercise:

Reflect on your life and relationships. Are you embodying truthfulness in every area of your life? Journal about this, paying special attention to anywhere you aren't being your most honest and authentic self.

Without judgment, write about any areas of misalignment and your feelings. What would be a more truthful expression of yourself in
those areas?

UNCONSCIOUS

The Unconscious card represents the vast, hidden depths of the mind that influence our thoughts, emotions, and behaviors. It symbolizes the unseen forces and

buried memories that shape our reality and impact our present experiences. This card invites you to explore the mysteries of your unconscious mind, bringing to light the hidden aspects of yourself that hold the key to greater self-awareness and transformation.

Key Meanings:

Hidden Influences: Hidden influences shape your thoughts and actions. Many of your behaviors and reactions stem from unconscious patterns and memories. By becoming aware of these hidden influences, you can begin to understand and transform them.

Inner Exploration: Engage in deep inner exploration and introspection. Delve into the recesses of your mind, uncovering buried emotions, desires, and fears. You can access the wisdom and insights held within your unconscious through meditation, journaling, or dream analysis.

Healing and Integration: Heal and integrate the hidden aspects of yourself. Confront and embrace your shadow side–the parts of yourself that you may have repressed or denied. By acknowledging and integrating these aspects, you achieve greater wholeness and self-acceptance.

Intuition: The unconscious is closely linked to intuition. Pay attention to the gut feelings that arise in your life. These intuitive insights can guide you toward deeper understanding and personal growth.

Takeaway:

Explore the hidden depths of your mind and bring awareness to the unconscious forces at play in your life. Engage in practices that foster introspection and self-discovery, allowing you to uncover and heal buried emotions and patterns. Trust your intuition and pay attention to what arises from your unconscious mind. By embracing the mysteries of
your inner world, you can achieve profound transformation and self-awareness.

Exercise:

Delve into your subconscious mind: spend a few minutes reflecting
on your dreams and any recurring symbols or themes before bed. Keep a dream journal to capture these insights, allowing your unconscious thoughts to reveal deeper truths and hidden desires.

WELLNESS

The Wellness card represents a state of holistic well-being, encompassing physical, mental, emotional, and spiritual health. It symbolizes the importance of nurturing every aspect of your being to achieve balance, vitality, and harmony. This card invites you to prioritize your wellness, listen to your body's needs, and adopt practices that promote overall health and well-being.

Key Meanings:

Physical Health: Prioritize your physical health by adopting practices that nourish and strengthen your body. Your body is the vessel through which you experience life and deserves your care and attention. By eating nutritious foods, engaging in regular physical activity, and ensuring adequate rest, you support your body's natural vitality and resilience.

Mental Clarity: Wellness includes maintaining mental clarity and emotional balance. Cultivate a healthy mindset by managing stress, practicing mindfulness, and engaging in activities that stimulate and challenge your mind. By taking care of your mental health, you enhance your ability to think clearly, make decisions, and easily navigate life's challenges.

Emotional Well-Being: Acknowledge and honor your emotions, allowing yourself to feel and express them healthily. By fostering emotional intelligence and resilience, you create a foundation of inner peace and stability that supports your overall well-being.

Spiritual Nourishment: Wellness also involves nurturing your spiritual self.

Connect with your higher self, explore your spiritual beliefs, and engage in practices that give you purpose and fulfillment. By nurturing your spiritual well-being, you create a sense of connection and harmony that enhances all other aspects of your life.

Takeaway:

Prioritize your holistic well-being. Listen to your body's needs, nurture your mind and emotions, and connect with your spiritual self.
Adopting practices that promote overall health and balance creates a foundation of vitality and harmony supporting your journey toward fulfillment and happiness.

Exercise:

Balancing Act

A sense of balance will help you enjoy overall wellness. First, stand with your feet 6 to 8 inches apart and close your eyes. Put all of your weight on your right foot. Then shift to the left foot and relieve the right foot completely. Do this back and forth 4 to 5 times, shifting your weight and paying attention to how it feels. After a few times of shifting right and left, stand with both feet on the ground. 50-50.

This exercise will promote better wellness by giving you more balance and stability, especially after you've isolated the left and right sides beforehand. You can do this anytime and anywhere. Try doing it every morning; a few weight shifts, and you'll feel ready to go.

Balancing Act in 4 Easy Steps

1. Stand with your feet 6 to 8 inches apart and close your eyes.
2. Put all your weight on your right foot, then your left foot. Notice how it feels.
3. Repeat 4 or 5 times.
4. Stand on both feet, centered and balanced.

WHOLENESS

The Wholeness card represents being complete, balanced, and harmonious within yourself. It embodies integrating all aspects of your being–mind, body, heart, and spirit–into a unified whole. This card invites you to recognize and celebrate your inherent completeness, embrace every part of yourself with love and acceptance, and cultivate a sense of inner harmony and peace.

Key Meanings:

Inner Harmony: Cultivate inner harmony by integrating all aspects of yourself. True wholeness comes from accepting and embracing every part of your being, including your strengths and weaknesses, light and shadow. Fostering self-acceptance and love creates a sense of inner peace and balance.

Self-Integration: Wholeness is about self-integration–bringing together the various parts of yourself into a cohesive and harmonious whole. Explore and honor the different facets of your personality, experiences, and emotions. By integrating these aspects, you better understand yourself and your unique journey.

Balance and Equilibrium: Remember the importance of balance and equilibrium in all areas of your life. Seek a balance between work and play, rest and activity, and giving and receiving. Creating a balanced lifestyle supports your overall well-being and cultivates a sense of wholeness.

Holistic Well-Being: Wholeness encompasses holistic well-being–nurturing your mind, body, heart, and spirit. Attend to all dimensions of your health, recognizing that each aspect contributes to your overall sense of completeness. You foster holistic well-being by caring for your physical, mental, emotional, and spiritual needs.

Takeaway:

Embrace and celebrate your inherent completeness. Cultivate inner harmony by integrating all aspects of yourself and seeking balance. Recognize that you are already whole and complete, just as you are.
By fostering self-acceptance, balance, and holistic well-being, you create a foundation of inner peace and harmony that radiates outwards into all areas of your life.

Exercise:

Speak this affirmation: "I am whole and complete, just as I am. I embrace all aspects of myself with love and acceptance and cultivate inner harmony and balance in all areas of my life."

WISDOM

The Wisdom card symbolizes the deep understanding and insight that comes from experience, introspection, and a connection to the higher truths of life. It represents the timeless and universal knowledge that guides us through our journey, helping us navigate challenges and make decisions aligned with our highest good. This card invites you to tap into your inner wisdom, trust your intuitive knowing, and seek the guidance that lies within and around you.

Key Meanings:

Inner Guidance: Trust your inner guidance and intuition. Within you lies a reservoir of wisdom that can guide you through life's complexities. By listening to your inner voice and paying attention to your intuitive nudges, you align yourself with the wisdom of your higher self.

Experience and Reflection: Wisdom is often born from experience and the reflections that follow. Look back on your past experiences with a discerning eye, recognizing the lessons learned and the growth achieved. By reflecting on your journey, you gain valuable insights that inform your present and future choices.

Seeking Knowledge: The Wisdom card emphasizes the importance of seeking knowledge and understanding and encourages you to be a lifelong learner, open to new ideas and perspectives. Whether through books, teachings, or conversations with wise individuals, the pursuit of knowledge enriches your life and broadens your horizons.

Balance and Discernment: Wisdom is about balance and discernment–

knowing when to act and when to wait, when to speak and when to listen. This card reminds you to approach situations with a balanced perspective, weighing the pros and cons, and considering the long-term implications of your decisions. By practicing discernment, you navigate life's challenges with grace and integrity.

Takeaway:

Trust the deep well of knowledge within you and seek guidance from both your inner self and external sources of wisdom. Reflect on your experiences, learn from them, and apply these lessons to your current situation. Embrace the journey of lifelong learning, and use your discernment to make decisions that align with your highest good. By tapping into your wisdom, you navigate life's path with clarity, confidence, and grace.

Exercise:

Quiet Moments

Sometimes, the best way to tap into our innate wisdom is to find a few moments of intentional quiet. Close your mouth with your lips just touching, your teeth slightly apart, and your tongue resting on the roof of your mouth. Sit very still like this, with your lips together, for a few moments. Soon, the quiet will begin. Your thinking and mind-chatter
will stop. All you need to do is observe.

Relaxing your mouth and jaw will quiet your mind and ease your stress, allowing your inner wisdom to be heard. Do this a few times when you need a quiet moment, and you'll soon find it happening automatically.

Quiet Moments in 3 Easy Steps

1. Close your mouth, lips just touching, teeth apart, and tongue resting on the roof of your mouth.
2. Sit still for a few moments and observe the stillness in your mind.
3. Observe your quieted mind and listen to your inner wisdom.

ZEN

The Zen card embodies tranquility, presence, and deep inner peace. It symbolizes the practice of mindfulness, the art of being fully present in the moment, and the pursuit of simplicity and balance in all aspects of life. This card invites you to cultivate a state of Zen by embracing stillness, letting go of distractions, and finding harmony within yourself and your surroundings.

Key Meanings:

Mindfulness: Practice mindfulness–being fully present and engaged in the here and now. You can find peace and clarity by paying attention to the present moment without judgment. Mindfulness allows you to experience life more
deeply and with greater appreciation.

Inner Peace: Zen represents the cultivation of inner peace and tranquility. Create a space of calm within yourself, regardless of external circumstances. By embracing practices such as meditation, deep breathing, and mindful movement, you can foster a state of inner serenity and balance.

Simplicity: There is beauty in simplicity. Simplify your life by letting go of unnecessary distractions, clutter, and complexity. By focusing on what truly matters and removing what does not, you create space for peace and harmony to flourish.

Balance and Harmony: Zen is about finding balance and harmony in all areas of your life. Seek equilibrium between work and rest, activity and stillness, and giving and receiving. By striving for balance, you create a fulfilling and sustainable life.

Takeaway:

Embrace mindfulness, simplicity, and inner peace. Practice being fully present in the moment to cultivate a state of inner tranquility and simplify your life by focusing on what truly matters. By embracing
the principles of Zen, you can create a life of balance, harmony, and profound peace.

Exercise:

Affirmation: "I embrace the tranquility within and around me, allowing inner peace to guide my thoughts, actions, and reactions."

RESOURCES ORIGINAL ACE Questionnaire

Prior to your 18th birthday:

1. **Did a parent or other adult in the household often or very often**

   Swear at you, insult you, put you down, or humiliate you?

   Or

   Act in a way that made you afraid that you might be physically hurt?

   Yes / No   If yes enter 1 _________

2. **Did a parent or other adult in the household often or very often**

   Push, grab, slap, or throw something at you?

   Or

   Ever hit you so hard that you had marks or were injured?

   Yes / No   If yes enter 1 _________

3. **Did an adult or person at least 5 years older than you ever**

   Touch or fondle you or have you touch their body in a sexual way?

   Or

   Attempt or actually have oral, anal, or vaginal intercourse with you?

   Yes / No   If yes enter 1 _________

4. **Did you often or very often feel that**

   No one in your family loved you or thought you were important or special?

   Or

   Your family didn't look out for each other, feel close to each other,
   or support each other?

   Yes / No   If yes enter 1 _________

5. **Did you often or very often feel that**

   You didn't have enough to eat, had to wear dirty clothes, and had no one to protect you?

   Or

   Your parents were too drunk or high to take care of you or take you to the doctor if you needed it?

   Yes / No   If yes enter 1 _________

6. **Were your parents ever separated or divorced?**

   Yes / No   If yes enter 1 _________

7. Was your mother or stepmother

Often or very often pushed, grabbed, slapped, or had something
thrown at her?

Or

Sometimes, often, or very often kicked, bitten, hit with a fist, or hit with something hard?

Or

Ever repeatedly hit over at least a few minutes or threatened with a
gun or knife?

Yes / No If yes enter 1 ________

8. Did you live with anyone who was a problem drinker or alcoholic, or who used street drugs?

Yes / No If yes enter 1 ________

9. Was a household member depressed or mentally ill, or did a household member attempt suicide?

Yes / No If yes enter 1 ________

10. Did a household member go to prison?

Yes / No If yes enter 1 ________

Now add up your "Yes" answers: ________
This is your ACE Score

11. Is there any additional stress, trauma, or damaging experience that has impacted you in some way? If so, please note it here.

12. Please go back and look at all of your "yes" responses. Write down the impact and effects those things have had on your life at the time, years, and decades later. After taking the ACE,
this one question has proven to be very helpful, important, and healing when people take the time to answer thoughtfully.

RESOURCES PCE Questionnaire

Prior to your 18th birthday:

1. **Did a parent or other adult in the household often or very often**

   Support, compliment, encourage, or show interest in your thoughts
   or concerns?

   Yes / No   If yes enter 1 _________

2. **Did a parent or other adult in the household often or very often**

   Hug, hold, read to you, or spend meaningful time with you?

   Yes / No   If yes enter 1 _________

3. **Did an adult or someone at least five years older than you ever**

   Take care of you, babysit, or tutor you in a kind and compassionate way while you were growing up?

   Yes / No   If yes enter 1 _________

4. **Did you often or very often feel that**

   Someone in your household loved you or thought you were important or special

   Or

   Your family looked out for each other, felt close, and supported each other?

   Yes / No   If yes enter 1 _________

5. **Did you often or very often feel that**

   You had enough to eat and clean clothes and had someone to protect you?

   Yes / No   If yes enter 1 _________

6. **Did your parents commonly**

   Show love or affection toward each other?

   Or

   Support, compliment, or hug each other in front of you?

   Yes / No   If yes enter 1 _________

7. **Did your mother or stepmother often or very often**

   Support or compliment you, or kiss or hug in front of you?

   Yes / No   If yes enter 1 _________

8. **Did you live with anyone who had a good sense of humor or was musical or artistic in any way?**

   Yes / No   If yes enter 1 ________

9. **Did a household member treat or communicate with your friends in a kind way?**

   Yes / No   If yes enter 1 ________

10. **Did a household member study new subjects, go to college, donate time to the community, or participate in fundraisers?**

    Yes / No   If yes enter 1 ________

Now add up your "Yes" answers: ________
This is your PCE Score

11. Are there any additional positive experiences that have impacted you in some way? If so, please note them here.

12. Please go back and look at all your "yes" responses and write down the impact and effects each of those things have had on your life. This approach has proven to be very helpful, important when people take the time to answer thoughtfully.

CONCLUSION

Thank you for embarking on this journey with the Oracle Card Deck. I sincerely hope this deck has been a source of insight, inspiration, and healing for you. Each card and exercise is designed to help you tap into your inner wisdom, confront and release past traumas, and build a resilient, empowered self.

The path to self-awareness and personal growth is a lifelong journey; these cards are meant to be your companions. As you continue to use this deck, you will uncover new layers of understanding and develop a deeper connection with your true self. Remember, the goal is not perfection but progress and self-acceptance.

By engaging with these cards, you take proactive steps toward a future filled with freedom, fulfillment, and joy. Each time you draw a card, reflect on its message, and practice the associated exercise,
you invest in your mental, emotional, and physical well-being.

The ACE Assessment in this booklet's "Resources" section is a valuable tool to further understand how your past experiences may influence your present. Use this knowledge as a stepping stone toward healing and transformation. By addressing and resolving past traumas, you can break free from their lingering effects and create a healthier, more vibrant future.

Your journey to becoming your own True Sage is unique and deeply personal. Trust the process, honor your progress, and be gentle with yourself. You have the power within you to transform your life, and this deck is here to support you every step of the way.

With gratitude and encouragement,

Dr. Alman
Founder, Clinical Director,
and CEO of True Sage

988 LIFELINE

Everyone needs to know that they can always get the help they need:

https://988lifeline.org | 988 Lifeline

At the 988 Suicide & Crisis Lifeline, they understand that life's challenges can sometimes be difficult.

Also by Dr. Brian Alman

1. Keep It Off
2. The Voice
3. The Voice for Kids
4. Self-Hypnosis
5. A Clinical Hypnosis Primer
6. Healthy Living Meditations
7. Your Inner Voice
8. Less Stress for Kids
9. Mind-Body Weight Loss
10. Less Stress Now
11. The 6 Steps to Freedom
12. Thin Meditations
13. Meditations to Lighten Up From the Inside Out
14. California Total Beauty
15. From Trauma to Enlightenment: The Four Steps to Unconditional Self-Acceptance

Additional titles from Dr. Brian Alman, published by Storyteller Media,
are available on www.storyteller.media:

From Trauma to Enlightenment

&

All Hypnosis is Self Hypnosis (Nov. 2026)

To explore more of Dr. Brian Alman's work, including the groundbreaking Enlightn App:

www.drbrianalman.com

Or by scanning the QR Code:

For media and booking inquiries:

contact@storyteller.media

ABOUT STORYTELLER PUBLISHING

At Storyteller Publishing, we believe stories are one of the last sacred spaces where people slow down, reconnect, and rediscover what matters most. Our mission is to champion voices with purpose, authors whose work inspires, challenges, heals, and invites readers to discover new worlds of imagination and truth.

Storyteller Publishing was founded by storytellers including bestselling authors, top publishers, and award-winning filmmakers who believe stories can change lives. We publish books that spark conversation, build bridges, and remind us that we are all connected by the human experience.

If our book found its way into your hands, we are honored. If it moved you in any way, even for a single sentence, we hope you will continue this journey with us.

Discover more books, authors, and upcoming releases at:

www.Storyteller.Media

For more on our films and television series:

www.Curiosity-Entertainment.com

For inquiries related to this author including media, speaking, or partnerships, contact us at: contact@Storyteller.Media

Join our community for new stories, merch drops from your favorite authors, special events, and behind-the-scenes updates:

Instagram: @StorytellerPublishing

TikTok: @TheStorytellerStore

Thank you for supporting our authors, our mission, and the stories that bring us all a little closer together.

Stories Live Here.